True Cow Tales
Literary Sketches and Stories by Farmers, Ranchers, and Dairy Princesses

D1519881

Edited by C. R. Lindemer
Foreword by SARA RATH, author of
The Complete Cow, About Cows, Dancing with a Cowboy,
and other books

First published by Dog Ear Publishing
4010 W. 86th Street, Ste H
Indianapolis, IN 46268
www.dogearpublishing.net

ISBN: 978-160844-061-0

This book is printed on acid-free paper.

Printed in the United States of America

Dedicated, with love,
to my husband and cattle aficionado,

Kevin J. Lindemer

ACKNOWLEDGMENTS

Thank you to supportive immediate and extended family members, and especially to Cathy Hartwig, Rita Stigsell, and to Leonard and Phyllis Bengtson, who are still operating a dairy farm in Minnesota.

A heartfelt thanks to the friends and the talented writers who have supported, encouraged, or inspired me in my writing and editing efforts: Patricia Axford, Sharon Briss, Peggy Chute, Prebble Eklof, Kathryn Leibowitz, Diane Margaretos, Kristen McEvoy, Georgess McHargue, Shirlee Morrison, Sandra Roschelle, Linda Saraco, Betty Taylor, and Jean Tennant.

The dairy princess chapter would not have been possible without the enthusiastic, gracious, and patient assistance of Char Hovland, Dairy Princess Coordinator for the Midwest Dairy Association. Also thank you to Marty Potts, Virginia Director – Dairy Princesses; Bev Lehs, Industry Relations Program Assistant for the Iowa Dairy Princess Program; Junia E. Isiminger, Executive Director for PA Dairy Princess & Promotion Services, Inc.; and Rae Ann Kelsch.

A special thank you for assistance from Kay Price and the August Derleth Society. And to Jean Jesensky, who helped me keep my business going while I was working on this project.

A belated thank you to my freshman college English professor, Sigurd K. Lee, for early encouragement in my writing.

And last but not least, I wish to acknowledge all of the farmers, ranchers, and dairy princesses who took the time to tell their stories and make this book possible.

FOREWORD

"When I was a kid we had this one cow named Mabel…" I can hear my husband launching into one of his farm stories, and I cringe because I know the city women at this dinner party will soon be rolling their eyes. "She was a huge cow, more the size of an ox than a regular dairy cow, with horns that came around the sides of her head. And she had really big teats." (Okay, there go the eyes.) "I mean they were *really* big. This big around." (He's gesturing here with thumb and forefinger.) "And about this long." (Can that really be 12 inches?) "And one day Mabel got into some brush where one of her teats got cut, and it was infected. Of course we milked by hand then, but she wouldn't let anyone get near her. My dad tried to milk her, and to keep her from kicking he put hobbles on her back feet. But she ended up kicking him with her *front* foot. So he left Mable for me to milk. I was the only one who could milk that cow without being kicked."

My husband had a hardscrabble childhood, growing up in a family of eight kids. Their father rented farms in Illinois, and they moved to a different one almost every spring after their dad purchased his first herd – *that one cow* was kept in their garage. You'd think these memories would be tinged with resentment, but when my husband's siblings get together they laugh so heartily while recalling their misadventures that I'm envious of the close bonds they shared growing up poor, working those rented farms.

Show me someone who doesn't love cows and I'll show you someone who turns up their nose at ice cream, won't eat a cheese pizza, hates chocolate milk, and doesn't appreciate the magnificent benefits of yogurt.

"Cows are the foster mother of the human race," Wisconsin's Governor William Dempster Hoard once said. He even had a notice posted in his barn: "Remember that this is the Home of Mothers. Treat each cow as a Mother should be treated."

I'll venture that no one included in this volume would argue with that point.

Beef cattle? I spent quality time during a sleet storm in Idaho with a gorgeous herd of Irish Dexters and their feisty little bull. Last July I shared a pasture with a herd of Scottish Highlanders as I admired their furry calves. Born and raised in Wisconsin, however, I am hard pressed to find anything more beautiful than a gathering of the girls — black and white Holsteins lying in shady green grass near a pasture creek on a sunny summer day.

I live in the country near Spring Green, Wisconsin – not far from famed architect Frank Lloyd Wright's Taliesin Studio. Wright was outspoken about cows, as he was on many subjects, but his personal philosophy is worth passing along. (Note: Wright was extremely fond of the color red.) "Wisconsin is a dairy state," he said. "That means herds of pure Holsteins or Guernseys, or what have you, occupying the best ground anywhere around, making pictures that go with the one made by the red barn. Wisconsin, fond of passing laws, should pass another law compelling every farmer to paint his barn red. Another that will compel him to pasture his cows by the highway and his pigs back behind the barn."

I have fallen in love with this collection of stories and poems that Christine Lindemer has gathered. In this volume you'll find stories of love and sorrow, of gentle cattle who nuzzled for hugs, and of farmers who had to give up their farms. Funny or sad, every story, every poem, has a genuine thread of love running through from beginning to end.

Unfortunately, the fate of our lovable cows is changing these days with the advent of factory farms that cram thousands of them together and insert chemicals to encourage higher milk production or larger sides of beef. Dolly and Bessie and Bossy are often identified only by numbers on the tags in their ears (or the bar code), and it's even likely that they're milked each day without the touch of a human hand.

I think of poor Mabel with her incredibly large and very sore teat – she wouldn't have enjoyed that at all.

Sara Rath

Introduction

For over half of my life, I've lived on farms and have spent a lot of time around cows, growing up on a dairy farm and now raising a few beef cattle. I've also lived in several U.S. states and cities, so I understand regional and cultural contrasts from "both sides of the fence."

What farmers and ranchers experience in their day-to-day lives may be completely unfamiliar to the person who carries a briefcase to an office building. A lot of what you do as a farmer or rancher, your knowledge and working traditions, was passed on to you by your farmer and rancher parents and grandparents.

Working with large domesticated animals has its familiar routines and comic episodes as well as dramas and dangers. Funny, touching, and scary things can happen, and most of those incidents never get reported past the immediate farming community.

In the winter of 2001, I began talking to my parents about cow stories from their childhoods and dairy farming careers. We each recalled a few stories of incidents involving cows and memories of favorite cows. And we knew there were many more such stories about cows across the country. Years later, I was able to collect enough stories to produce this collection.

Prepare yourself to enter a world of hairy heifers, beastly bulls, cute calves, and their hard working and interesting owners. These folks wanted you to know what it's really like to work with cattle and live and work on farms and ranches. You just might be surprised.

Some kind and lovely dairy princesses were also generous enough to share their stories. And I am awestruck by the fact that I can say I have spoken and corresponded with "the butterhead lady," who carves the world-renowned dairy princess butter sculptures for the Minnesota State Fair. I never imagined that I'd get past that glassed-in refrigerated case.

C. R. Lindemer

CONTENTS

Favorite Cows

Dixie and Dawn 3
    Shirley Ann (Brown) Gummer

"Hoogey" 7
    Kermit H. Dietrich

My Three Jerseys 9
    L. Betty Dietrich

Roland's "Sugar" 11
    Diane Popenhagen

A Mother's Day Surprise 17
    Marion Greveling

"Grazielle" the Spirited Cow 21
    J. Daniel Rohrer

"Traktor" 23
    Helen Meadows

A Story about "Sally" and Milk and Cookies 31
    Kermit H. Dietrich

Tales by 4-H'ers

4-H 35

Oreo Cookies and a 4-H Moment! 37
    Helen Meadows

"Fairground Fancy" 41
    Terrell Timmons

Halter Breaking "CC"...................................43
    Cathy Thomas

Bovine Drama

"Ferdy" 49
    Tiffany McMillan

The Bull . . . and I..55
    Roger Stoner

Saving Polly's Life 61
    Robert Stewart

Bull-headed Bull...63
    Chuck G. Hosford

Bovine Protection Squad 67
    Sheila Paquet

"Hunter"..71
    Helen Meadows

Dairy Princesses

About Dairy Princesses of the U.S 83

The First Princess Kay of the Milky Way 87
    Eleanor Maley Thatcher

The Butterhead Sculptor..93
     Linda Christensen

Who Inspired the Butter Carton Skirt?.......................97
     Donna Moenning

The North Dakota Dairy Queen of 1951 101
     Shirley Ann (Brown) Gummer

Iowa's First Dairy Princess 105
     Dolores Chapman–Tanner

May Day Ruse 109
     Karen Bright Carey

Grandma's Miracle 113
     Shelby Bohnenkamp

2007 Princess Kay of the Milky Way 121
     Ann Miron

The "Dear Dairy" in my Life.....................................125
     Amanda Messick

Milking Cows with the I-Cubs 129
     Jennifer Zumbach

Living my Childhood Dream......................................131
     Merideth (Weiderspahn) Riddle

Cattle Sillies

The Heifer That Rolled Me 139
     Hank Pool

How to Feed the Chickadees in Winter 141
     Marion Greveling

Close Encounters: Alvin & Margie 145
    Kermit H. Dietrich

Bull at Play 147
    Becky Iciek

Cow Poetry

The Cow 151
    Ogden Nash

The New Cow...152
    August Derleth

You See an Old Barn 153
    Linda Schumacher

The Cow 155
    Robert Louis Stevenson

Teaching a Calf to Drink 156
    Anonymous

The 4-H Show..158
    Ivan N. Gates

Cow Haikus 159
    C. R. Lindemer

Cattle Escapes

Ole "Red" 163
    Clint Kepferle

Shoot to Kill 167
    J. Daniel Rohrer

Lulu's Big Day..173
    As told by Lauri D. Goldenhersh

Columbus Day, 1997 181
    C. R. Lindemer

Bovine Wistfulness

Milking Cows in Iowa 187
    Arlene Stratman Walker

Warming Your Feet, "Country Style" 193
    Kermit H. Dietrich

Hilja and Ed's Place..195
    Robert Darling

Learning to Walk 199
    Allen Doyle

Always a Cowgirl...201
    Verda Vanecek Doop

Favorite Cows

Whoever needs milk, bows to the animal.

~ Yiddish saying

Dixie and Dawn

Shirley Ann (Brown) Gummer

North Dakota Dairy Queen of 1951

My two favorite cows were sisters. One was very light colored, almost beige, and the other was a very dark brown. Dixie and Dawn were beautiful Brown Swiss cows with big brown eyes that would light up every time they saw me. They were always winning the blue ribbons or Grand Champion titles at the fairs. Dixie was trained so well that she would respond to me through commands. She wore a halter during parades; however, I never held onto it. The crowds were always in awe.

Brown Swiss cattle have personalities widely known to be very passive and gentle. Dixie and Dawn followed me around, and I literally had to push them aside. Sometimes, they were more of a nuisance. Both of them expected hugs from me, nuzzling and pushing until I gave them some love.

I worked hard on the farm, helping my dad with the cattle and in the field. Part of my pay was my two beautiful friends, Dixie and Dawn. These two heifers brought a great deal of fame to the Elm Bend Farm in Blanchard, North Dakota, due to how well they were trained and the consistently high awards they won at the fairs and shows.

Every Saturday and Sunday was devoted to teaching the cows to lead. Our family usually showed around 25 head of cattle at the fairs. And because of my successes with Dixie and Dawn, my dad thought I should train all of the cows. My brother thought that was a great idea too!

When I would ride my horse out to the pasture to bring the cows in for milking, Dixie and Dawn would come running to see me and would walk right beside me and my horse all the way to the barn. Most of the time I would just call their names, and they would come on their own to the barn, leading the rest of the herd.

Dawn was the one that loved to run up the cattle ramp into the truck. She knew she was going to a fair. They both loved to get a bath when we were getting ready for show day. When they were in the show ring, they were the show-offs. They would plant their feet perfectly and stand or show to perfection. Judges always commented on their showmanship, wondering if I even had to work at all!

One year when I was at the State Dairy Show in Jamestown, Dixie was about to have a calf. I was showing her, and she was getting more and more anxious by the minute. She did receive a Grand Champion award, and it was just in the nick of time. We were not back at her stall 10 minutes when her baby calf appeared. She had a beautiful little heifer, and I named her Miss Jimmie because she was born in Jamestown.

Dixie and Dawn were treated like the family pets. They used to roam the farmyard like the cats and dogs. They never bothered anything, just demanded attention. When they died, they were 13 and 17 years old, respectively. Both of them were buried on the family farm, right next to the loyal family dogs. It was such a sad time for me, because they truly were such great pets and had provided me with many years of fun and companionship.

Shirley Ann (Brown) Gummer and her husband raised beef cattle and small grains in North Dakota until 1999. She has five grandchildren and one great-grandchild. She has been active as a cattle judge and a princess judge and serves as the Chairman of the North Dakota State Milk Marketing Board.

"Hoogey"
Kermit H. Dietrich

"Hoogey" was born in South Dakota in 1933, so named by my parents, Carl and Kathrine, because I couldn't say "Holstein."

Hoogey was shipped by rail to Louisiana with the rest of our livestock and machinery, and after two tough years, back north to the Wiedenbach farm at Lake Sarah in Loretto, Minnesota. Two years later she went with us to the Dongoski farm near Lyndale, Minnesota. Her last home was the Kruger farm in Greenfield, which was the first farm that Pa bought.

Ma always helped with the milking, so my older brother, Ernie, and I came down to the barn, from early childhood, and wanted to be helpers. Hoogey was "my" first cow, as she was gentle and an "easy milker."

My early enthusiasm quickly wore off. I was up by 6:00 a.m., went to the warm and humid barn, sat on a little three-legged stool, and put my head against Hoogey's warm belly. I quickly fell asleep before much milk was produced.

Years later, when I had a large dairy herd, Ma shook her head in wonder that I had become a dairy farmer.

To this day, I can think of nothing more peaceful than hand-milking cows, feeling the warmth of the cows, and listening to the rhythm of the streams of milk hitting the bottom of a metal pail.

Kermit H. Dietrich is a retired dairy farmer and U.S. Navy submarine veteran living in Waconia, Minnesota. He has taught English as a Second Language and currently volunteers at the Carver County Historical Museum. He is now an artist and enjoys painting.

The Dietrich Dairy Farm in 1975 in Maple Plain, Minnesota.
Photo courtesy of L. Betty Dietrich.

My Three Jerseys
L. Betty Dietrich

When I was a teenager, I was given a Jersey calf for my own. Jerseys are very beautiful and gentle animals. They are golden with dark eyes, and the milk they produce is very rich.

My Jersey calf's name was Prudence. I raised her from the time she was a calf. When Prudence grew up, she had a heifer calf that I named "Trudy." Most of the time, Trudy was raised in a calf pen. Sometimes I would let her out of the pen and she would follow me around the yard, just like a frisky puppy. When Trudy grew up, she gave me another heifer calf. All of these three Jersey cattle became part of my parents' dairy herd.

When I married the farm boy next door, Kermit H. Dietrich, on June 4, 1954, he was surprised when my parents led the three Jersey cattle from their farm to ours. He called them my "dowry."

We raised most of our herd replacement cows, but occasionally bought a few cows at livestock auctions. We operated our dairy farm from June of 1954 until May of 1993. In May of 1993 we sold our dairy cows to several local farmers. The remaining heifers were sold by September of 1994. They were trucked to Princeton, St. Paul, and Zumbrota, Minnesota.

We did enjoy our 39 dairy years on the farm.

L. Betty Dietrich is a retired dairy farmer living in Waconia, Minnesota. She is the mother of three daughters and the grandmother to eight children. Betty enjoys bird watching, "classic" movies, and painting. She is a former student of artist Ken Zylla.

Grandma P.'s Corncrib © C. R. Lindemer

Roland's "Sugar"

Diane Popenhagen

Roland didn't mind the solitude. Each morning he left the warm breathing of his wife, Carol, to don his cold, stiff denim overalls. By the time Carol walked into the small kitchen, he had already eaten his oatmeal and toast and was grabbing his favorite cap, with its bill curled just right after years of wear. He kissed her good-bye and headed to "Old Red," his faithful Chevy pickup, which was encrusted with rust and dried mud.

As Roland opened the front door on this morning, the cold seemed fiercer than in his 36 years of farming. The wind stole his breath away. Through his heavy overalls, Roland could feel the penetrating cold of the seat beneath him. He knew he would arrive at the barn long before his body warmth would have any effect on the vinyl beneath him or the cold steering wheel.

"Old Red's" lights shone on his old place. Roland and Carol had moved to a smaller house down the road a few years back. They thought the change would make their lives better in some way, but it had only resulted in adding a five-minute drive twice every day.

The glint of the cows' eyes shone as the headlights caught their gaze in the early morning darkness. Roland turned off the choking engine of the truck and sat in silence. He could hear the slow shuffle of cattle's hooves as they started to move toward the barn. His coarse voice called them to their morning milking, "Here, cow. Here, cow."

He opened the sliding barn door and watched the procession that started every day he had known since his youth and heard the lowing of the cattle as they shuffled to their spots. Each cow knew her space and found comfort in the routine. Although silent workmanship would have been sufficient, Roland spoke to each cow as he hooked on the milkers.

"Now, Shelly, you be still now. I warmed my hands, so this should go easy." He stroked her back as she turned her head to make brief eye contact.

"Dinah, I'm standing on your left, so I expect no complaints now, you hear?"

One by one, he hooked them up to the milking machines. All of them, except for Sugar. He called her "Sugar" because her milk was as sweet as honey, but she was particular and only wanted to be milked by hand. Roland didn't mind so much, as it gave him something to do as the milking machines were running.

"Sugar, you ready?" He sat down on the milking stool, worn through by his unique form. His calloused hands were rough but gentle on Sugar's udder. The warm milk steamed in the cold metal bucket.

Roland laid his world-weary head against Sugar's flank. He breathed deeply to delay his tears. "Sugar, I'm sorry," he choked, as he continued to milk her. "I tried the best I could." He felt foolish as the words left his mouth. Why was he trying to explain the ways of man to an animal?

For months he had tried to fight the government standards, which were set so far out of the common man's reach. He had watched as small dairy farms collapsed under the weight of regulations set by "men in suits," far removed from the earth beneath his fingernails.

"I wanted them to keep your name, Sugar! I didn't want them to give you a number! I'm so sorry. I know you don't understand this, but I'm so sorry," he quietly wept as he leaned against her one last time.

He dried his tears with a sleeve of his flannel shirt as he began the process of releasing the cows one last time. He removed the milkers, and the cows slowly sauntered back out to the pasture. He plodded to the adjoining milk room to inspect the milk in its labyrinthine steel tank. The white liquid pool swirled against the paddle, around and around, within the cold stainless steel.

Roland checked the pressure gauges and returned for the solitary bucket of Sugar's milk. At the barn's threshold, Roland was surprised to see his bovine friend had not yet made her way out of the barn.

"Now, Sugar, you get on now," Roland said as he gave her a gentle shove. He watched her turn slowly, resistant to leave.

He put a lid on the milk bucket to bring home to Carol. Then he secured the gate to the pasture and turned away. The gravel shifted unpredictably under his feet as he made his way back to "Old Red." He turned to look over his shoulder as he backed up and turned around to head back home. His weathered hand adjusted the rearview mirror to reflect the entire herd of 28 cows.

As he drove away, the dust obscured his view. Roland fought to face all that was real and to relinquish that which was already gone. He had never been one to think much about himself, so he was ill equipped to face this theft of his life's definition and the bargain price bid for his identity.

When he returned to his farmhouse, his eyes studied the familiar boards of the aged, wooden floor. He was there much too early for a full day's work. Roland continued to the kitchen, and Carol silently approached him. She reached up to his worried and weathered face with her small, soft hands. He searched her pale blue eyes for any lack of respect or loss of loyalty.

He had lost the farm.

But he saw only tenderness and compassion and was immediately thankful for her constancy, which was becoming the only reliable currency in his possession.

"Mama, you want some milk?" Roland asked his wife.

"Let me get some glasses down," Carol replied, quickly turning to open the chipped, painted wood cabinets.

They went out to the screened porch to escape the confines of the small country house. There they sat, side by side, with glasses full of warm milk, as they watched the empty road stretch out before them.

"She's still as sweet as she ever was, Papa," Carol commented on the thick froth of Sugar's milk.

"She sure is, Mama. She sure is."

Diane Popenhagen has enjoyed a successful career as a magazine columnist, author, and editor. She divides her time between project managing and editing for a small book publisher, running a thriving ghostwriting firm, and keeping up with her three children, two dogs, two doves, and a conure . . . not to mention her husband! Roland's "Sugar" was based on her Uncle Roland's fight to keep his small dairy in Canton, Minnesota.

A Mother's Day Surprise

Marion Greveling

As a young girl, my preferred place to be was on my Uncle Lloyd and Aunt Bette's farm. At that time they bred Polled Herefords. Those red and white cattle were my favorite breed, especially the young calves. Those white faces with big, soft eyes surrounded by long eyelashes that any girl would envy were irresistible to my animal-crazy heart. I loved to watch them frisking about in the pasture fields, kicking their heels up and running full out, their tails seeming to steer them along.

I loved the soft feel of a newborn calf and the sound of a calf nursing noisily at her mother's udder. At that time I had no idea of the hard work and long hours that came along with farming. I only saw the freedom that I had there, the long lazy hours of playing in the hay mow, building hay forts, and finding new kittens. I wanted to know everything there was to know about animals and had the dream of many young girls that I would grow up to be a veterinarian.

As it turned out, I did not go to veterinary school. I did, however, end up married to a man who shared many of the same interests, especially when it came to animals and farm work. Lawrence and I were able to buy a piece of land, and after a few years we began building a farm of our own and a home for ourselves and our four children.

I had often spoken to my family about the days on my aunt and uncle's farm. One May day, Lawrence found me out working in the garden and said he wanted to show me something. He didn't say just what he wanted to show me, but invited me to come along in the truck with him and our grinning children.

We drove a few miles down the road to the farm of a man whom my husband had worked for when he was a teenager. We got out of the truck and walked back to the barn. As we walked, my husband told me that Bill had invited him to stop by sometime to see his cattle.

As we came around the corner, I saw an assortment of cattle, but my eye was drawn to the Herefords among them. We talked about the different animals and which ones we liked best. Lawrence then told me that since Mother's Day was coming up, he and the children thought I should pick two of those Hereford heifers to come home with us. I was so surprised - - I had never expected this at all! I happily chose two of those beautiful bovines, and Bill promised to deliver them as soon as our fencing was finished.

The kids wanted to know what I would call our new heifers. I laughed and said that one would be "Patty" (Cow Patty, of course!) and the other, "Paige." They were the best Mother's Day present I could have wished for. No television commercial ever prompted men, sons, and daughters to buy livestock for their wives or mothers—but I'm sure glad that my family thought of it!

That event took place 13 years ago now. Patty died four years ago, after her stomach twisted, but her daughter "Loretta" is a "spitting image" of her. Paige is still here at the farm and raises a fine calf every year. Our herd will never be large, but they will always be part of our farm, and when I see those new calves every year, they remind me of the carefree times of my youth and the happiness of those days.

Marion Greveling lives in Ontario, Canada, on a dairy sheep farm with her husband, four children, and ruminant animals, both large and small. She enjoys gardening, making sheep's milk cheese, and attending the local farmer's market.

"Grazielle" the Spirited Cow

J. Daniel Rohrer

We had a beef cow a few years ago that was part Chianina. She was a gray beast with horns. We called her "Grazielle." ("Gratte-ciel" means "skyscraper" in French, and she was a jumper!) She was the most curious animal around, coming right up to you and sniffing around. But make a move toward her and she was gone like a deer!

We tried one time to move her from one farm to another to check 'em, but she squirted away through three-line fences and into the neighbor's field. By the time we got the other cattle loaded, she was right back where she belonged. We decided then and there that she was a "lifer" for our farm. There was just no way to get rid of her.

Spring came a few years back, and Grazielle was heavy with calf. I got up one morning to check the cows and found them all over the place. Upon further examination, I found Grazielle lying dead at the edge of the pasture.

You'll never convince me that in the throes of a heart attack or some other such fatal ailment, Grazielle didn't struggle over the fence and try to take it down with her last gasp so those other cows could go free.

We still have a few of her crazy offspring running around the place, including a whitish-gray great-granddaughter that my daughter calls "Bianca"......I wonder if she can fly.......

When he's not chasing cows, **Dan Rohrer** lives with his wife and daughter, as well as their German Shepherd and tri-colored cat, on a small farm outside of Watertown, Wisconsin. He farms as "a hobby" with his father and uncle, and raises beef cattle, chickens, cucurbits, corn, soybeans, and alfalfa.

"Traktor"

Helen Meadows

At the Meadows Ranch that evening, things were in an uproar. Calving season was in full swing, and a heifer by the name of Meadowlark was in labor. She was a bit wild so Bill and Helen made preliminary preparations, setting up temporary fences to guide the cattle on their way into the corral. A fine spring drizzle poured from the darkened overhead clouds.

The herd moved quickly to the first gate, and Meadowlark, surprisingly, walked right into the corral. With a few quick maneuvers she was secured in the round pen. Bill's initial exam in the squeeze chute revealed that the heifer's hips were too narrow for calving unassisted. Helen phoned the veterinarian in Hot Springs, and drove in the waning evening light up Big Beaver Road to fetch Wilma, the heifer's owner, so she could watch the cesarean section.

Clearly Meadowlark was agitated at being confined in the squeeze chute. For one startling moment, she recognized Wilma and licked her hand. Under a steady rain, Helen held a flashlight and Bill held some of the internal organs as he assisted the vet with the surgery. Soon a healthy bull calf was delivered. He was a warm brown color with a white blaze on his head.

After the anesthetic wore off, Meadowlark was not happy. She had "management issues." She didn't like Bill and Helen, didn't like being at their ranch, and the discovery of a new calf only agitated her more. She kicked the newborn, and no maternal instincts settled in. The calf looked lost and wandered away from the corral, away from his mother, to a safer place.

Because another cow, Meadowbrook, had recently lost her calf, Bill thought this newborn could be grafted onto her. But it didn't happen. Meadowbrook cared for the calf about as much as Meadowlark did.

Meadowlark was locked in the squeeze chute so Bill could milk her. Held captive in this manner, it was possible for the calf to nurse without being injured by his mother. Because this was her first calf, and she had been sedated during delivery, she didn't claim it. So Bill and Helen developed a daily routine. Bill milked Meadowlark, pouring the warm milk into the waiting bottle to be fed to the calf. Occasionally the calf actually nursed at his mother's udder. These occasions were a joy to watch. The calf butted Meadowlark's udder and sucked vigorously.

About a week later, Meadowlark developed symptoms of illness and showed signs of stress. Her milk supply dwindled until it disappeared entirely. The infection that took away her milk developed her management issues even more. At that point, no one could get within yards of her. Head high, eyes glazed, she was as set to explode as a stick of dynamite in a barrel of gasoline.

Faithfully, Helen brought the calf's nourishment twice a day, while Bill searched for someone to take the calf. He called friends who might be interested in a healthy bottle-fed calf. He heard rumors that day-old calves were selling for up to $300 dollars back at the livestock auction, but there were no offers for this particular calf.

Bill thought that if they were going to keep the calf for awhile, they should name him. Helen suggested the name "Meadow-will," after their last name, Meadows, and Wilma, the calf's owner.

Late one afternoon as Helen stepped outside, the calf, seeing Helen and thinking "supper," climbed up the three steps to the porch. He made click-clack sounds on the wood as he investigated this new place. While Helen was wondering how on earth she was going to move him off the porch, she heard a noisy "kerplunk." The calf had somehow walked outside the porch railing when he made a misstep, landing on the grass below.

The calf learned quickly when it was feeding time. He became predictable, wandering up to the house at 8:00 a.m. and 5:00 p.m. The calf eventually had the run of the ranch.

The flower beds were his first play area, then the lawn. He seemed to think he was a person. As mealtime approached, he walked onto the concrete slab by the patio door and peered in. He dribbled slobber all over the glass after he finished eating, and he followed Helen as though she were his mother. Sal, the farm dog, did her best to lick and play with the calf.

One late afternoon, the dark brown UPS truck pulled into the driveway. After placing a parcel into Helen's hands, the delivery man turned to go. The calf emerged from the tulip bed near the garage and ambled up to investigate the visitor. A look of surprise and pleasure crossed the man's face at this unexpected sight. "That made my day!" he exclaimed.

A week later, as Helen visited with her daughter, Maria, about "the calf," Maria asked why the calf was never called by name. The name Meadow-will had never caught on. Somewhere in the conversation, it was decided to let two-year-old grandson, Benjamin, name the calf. His favorite toy was a green tractor, so "Traktor" the calf, spelled as Benjamin pronounced it in his Southern way, came into being.

The day came, however, when Traktor wanted to be with his own kind. After he sucked down the remains of his bottle, he turned and slowly walked through the wide open field, in search of the herd. Watching from the kitchen window, Helen felt as if one of her children was leaving for kindergarten the first time. She thought, "I hope he'll be okay." Although he frolicked with the other calves, he was back at the gate in time for his evening feeding.

Traktor learned his name and quickly came when called, or he'd start mooing whenever he saw Helen. Spindly when young, the special formula began to work, and he developed a healthy appetite. He often watched for the back door to open and for someone to appear with his food.

One time, in his eagerness, he jerked at the bottle with enough force to pull the rubber nipple off. The nipple was still in his mouth, like an enlarged pacifier, the bottle off to one side in the grass, milk dribbling out. Traktor looked puzzled, and did it again. The third time it happened, he seemed to learn and wasn't so aggressive, After his first bottle was empty, he sucked impatiently on the bottom corner of the container, then chased the tabby cat out, as though she were responsible for preparing his dinner. He butted the big rubber-tipped bottle as if it were the cow's udder. In his greed to eat, he hovered too close, and his sharp hoof ground into Helen's baby toe. "Ouch!"

For the next feeding Helen stayed on one side of the fence and angled the bottle on a metal slat of the gate so Traktor could drink from the other side. When he finished, he turned back in the direction from which he came, his belly swollen like a giant toadstool after a spring rain.

Traktor lived up to his name - - he plowed through fences to get to wherever he wanted to go. The electric fence didn't stop him from coming and going as he pleased. He mysteriously managed to escape through any fence on the ranch.

One evening a pickup truck drove in, and Traktor raced along the fence line, trying to outrun the diesel engine. The next evening Traktor wanted to be with the herd, but couldn't figure out how they got up on the hillside to graze. He had never walked through the tunnel that went underneath the county road, so he wandered out on the road. Bill lifted the barbed wire strands and poked him through. Morning came, and the cattle moved off the hillside for a drink. Traktor again didn't understand the tunnel, so paced the fence line, moving farther and farther away from the rest of the group. Finally, Helen called his name, walked to the fence, and let him climb back through.

The herd was in a rotational grazing system, moving to a new pasture every three days. Always the last animal to leave, Traktor walked with Bill and Helen, as if he weren't a bovine at all, but another person helping move the livestock.

When some relatives visited with their motor home and parked in the camping spot, Traktor took it upon himself to be their official morning greeter. They were amused and charmed by the little guy who suddenly appeared from around the corner, curiously sniffed their vehicle, and stayed outside the door until he was noticed.

One day Helen closed the kitchen door, walked down the steps, opened the car door, and started the engine. Traktor watched with interest, crawled through the fence and bounded over to the passenger side, where he stuck his head in through the open window. His cow breath seemed to ask, "Isn't it time to eat?"

In the social order of the cattle, he was an outcast. The cows pushed and shoved him as he tried to drink from the water tank. Undiscouraged, he simply crawled through the electric fence to the other side, where he could drink without interruption. The cows would circle about him curiously as his evening bottle was brought out. Occasionally, a cow would reach out and lick his face.

As summer continued, a predictable course was set. Visitors were impressed when Traktor came running when his name was called, and later took turns holding his nightly bottle. Helen and Bill's daughter, Maria, and her son, Benjamin, enjoyed feeding the tame critter with the dark, gentle eyes and the sweet scent of grass on his breath.

When the family reunion arrived, each of the young children learned the technique of holding Traktor's bottle. Because he was nearing 300 pounds, they all had to be careful he didn't crush their feet or knock them over.

One late summer afternoon Traktor appeared from "out of nowhere" and started making a nuisance of himself as the family embarked on a hayride. Pacing alongside the trailer, and annoying the group as they climbed aboard, it was evident that he wanted to be included in the festivities. Abruptly, Traktor lowered his head like a left tackle in the final seconds of a championship football game, poised to take on all challengers, and headed for cousin Kerry. With his quick reflexes, Kerry agilely stepped to the side, out of his reach. This was the first indication that the calf wasn't a cute little pet any more, but a growing bullock that could no longer be trusted to roam about as he pleased.

A short while later a pen made of hog panels put an end to Traktor's Houdini-like escapes. Try as he might, he couldn't wedge more than his head through the boards and woven wire. As Helen walked past to feed the chickens, he mooed, pleading to be let out. Bill dumped some corn and pellets into a rubber feed bucket, and before long this new item on his menu replaced his longing for milk.

The fall day arrived when Traktor was sent back to Wilma's ranch. He bounded into the trailer without hesitation and was soon on his way without a backward glance, disappearing forever, leaving only the memories he created for the family who had cared for him.

Helen Meadows is a native Montanan and grew up on a farm near Corvallis, Montana. She graduated from Montana State University with a B.S. in Home Economics, and volunteered for over 25 years as 4-H leader and culinary judge at the County Fair. Helen and her family currently raise Simmental/Red Angus cattle on their ranch in Sanders County, Montana.

A Story about "Sally" and Milk and Cookies

Kermit H. Dietrich

In the early '40s, an elderly farm couple moved into a rented house across from our farm. August and Mrs. Zitzloff had lost their farm during the Depression and were living on a small pension and handyman jobs.

They had a small Guernsey cow named "Sally." Sally grazed the roadsides and was smart enough to stay out of the cropland. August took his pail to Sally and milked her where he found her. We would see them early in the morning, this large old man milking a cow at the roadside.

Afternoons, Sally lay under a tree in their yard, chewing her cud. The neighborhood kids would sit on her and pet her.

When Sally was "fresh," she gave more milk than the Zitzloff's could drink and churn into butter. August poured the excess into our cans, which were at the end of the drive-way waiting for pickup.

They had Sally for two years. After she was gone, one day my folks sent me over with a Mason jar of milk. When Mrs. Zitzloff offered to pay, Pa said, "No, this is to pay back what Sally gave us."

I delivered a jar of milk several times a week, and with each delivery I received a large sugar cookie as a reward. This continued even through my high school years. The day I left for the Navy, I delivered my last quart. I ate the cookie on the train in Kansas on the way to boot camp.

****

Both August and Mrs. Zitzloff died while I was in the service, both in the same week.

Kermit H. Dietrich is a retired dairy farmer and U.S. Navy submarine veteran living in Waconia, Minnesota. He has taught English as a Second Language and currently volunteers at the Carver County Historical Museum. He is now an artist and enjoys painting.

Kermit H. Dietrich in his milking parlor.
Photo courtesy of L. Betty Dietrich.

Tales by 4-H'ers

"Beef, milk, butter, and cream:
four products from the farms of the American Dream."
~ An American farmer

4-H

The 4-H Youth Development Program, administered by 4-H National Headquarters, Cooperative State Research, Education, and Extension Service of the United States Department of Agriculture, originated in the U.S. around the beginning of the 20th century.

The name "4-H," symbolized by a four-leaf clover, stands for Head, Heart, Hands, and Health. The official 4-H emblem is green with white *H*'s on each leaf – the 4-H colors.* The white symbolizes purity. The green represents nature's most common color and is emblematic of youth, life, and growth.

The 4-H motto is "To make the best better." And the slogan of the program is "Learn by doing" (or, alternatively, "Learn to do by doing").

The 4-H program is the outreach of the Land Grant University System to our youngest citizens. Originally an agriculturally-focused organization, 4-H's Mission Mandates are citizenship; healthy living; and engineering, science, and technology (SET). The 4-H Youth Development Program strives to develop skills in these areas through experiential learning programs.

Over six million youth members are currently served in the U.S. More than 80 countries have created a youth development program like 4-H; these programs operate independently, as there is no international 4-H organization. However, through international exchanges, global education programs, and communications, they share a common bond in the shared values of 4-H.

The 4-H pledge is:

"I pledge my head to clearer thinking,

My heart to greater loyalty,

My hands to larger service

And my health to better living,

For my club, my community, my country, and my world."

* The 4-H Name and Emblem are federally protected under 18 U.S.C. 707. Use of the 4-H Name in this book does not imply endorsement of any commercial endeavor.

Oreo Cookies and a 4-H Moment!

Helen Meadows

For as long as she could remember, my daughter Renita had anticipated this time of her life: autumn fair time and being 11 years old – finally old enough to compete in "4-H" with her very own cow, Ruby. Renita had worked and saved all of her birthday money for five years until the amount grew to $825, enough to purchase a purebred Simmental heifer.

The entry blank had been carefully penciled in - - Class 23, Lot 4, Breeding Beef, Female, Two years or older - - and turned in to the Fair Office on time. The registration certificate showing the pedigree was tucked into a manila envelope and placed with the exhibitor tags.

As the fair approached, Renita packed feed, pitchforks, shovels, and water buckets. I stocked a corner of the tack box with the treats reserved for special occasions: a six-pack of soda, red licorice, green grapes, and a box of Oreo cookies.

The late August day of the fair was perfect. The fairgrounds were looking their best. The grass was a deep, rich green, mowed close as a crew cut, and dotted with old-fashioned wooden picnic tables. Carnival rides cartwheeled in the sky. Pickups and horse trailers rattled along. The grounds smelled like a cafeteria - - deep-fried corndogs and sweet cotton candy - - and swarmed like a beehive as spectators and competitors bustled about.

At 10:00 a.m., when the first Beef Class was scheduled for judging, the crowd settled back in anticipation. The Barn Superintendent went into his regular "spiel," reminding the kids to pin their numbers on their backs and be ready when their lot was called, a repeat of what had been heard earlier.

Renita stood with Ruby, freshly groomed and standing by her side, ready to waltz into the show ring. She day-dreamed about winning a blue ribbon as she adjusted her blue jeans over her cowboy boots, tucked in her white shirt, removed the scotch comb from her hip pocket, and brushed Ruby's hair once more.

Cow and girl trod together across a stretch of grass into the sawdust-covered arena. On the bleachers, a gathering of parents, 4-H leaders, and youngsters created a kaleidoscope of brilliant colors and moving shapes against the blue clear sky.

The cattle were paraded in a circle, set up, and walked again under the judge's scrutinizing eye. He checked their overall appearance for balance and eye appeal. He looked up, then down at his papers, carefully jotting down notes. Finally, having reached a decision, he headed for the announcer's stand.

"The little cowgirl with the Simmental cow gets a blue ribbon!" declared the judge.

Applause erupted, and a jubilant smile swept upon Renita's face as she accepted the silky blue First Place ribbon.

Then, with ribbon streaming and head high, she led the way, shouldering around with a cluster of well-wishers.

"Ruby, I love you," she whispered, reaching up and pressing her cheek to the cow and then planting a kiss in the same spot. As a further expression of her affection, she dug into the tack box and pulled out a handful of Oreo cookies that she fed to Ruby!

Onlookers dropped their jaws in astonishment at the cookie-eating heifer, as Ruby beamed with pride for her hard-earned ribbon. It was a "4-H moment."

Reprinted with permission of AgriNews Publications

Helen Meadows is a native Montanan and grew up on a farm near Corvallis, Montana. She graduated from Montana State University with a B.S. in Home Economics, and volunteered for over 25 years as 4-H leader and culinary judge at the County Fair. Helen and her family currently raise Simmental/Red Angus cattle on their ranch in Sanders County, Montana.

"Fairground Fancy"

Terrell Timmons

My sister Polly had a cow that she always showed in 4-H. Her name was Fancy. Fancy was a Holstein with a white face marking that looked like the letter *F*.

Polly started showing Fancy at the Geauga County Fair in Burton, Ohio, when she was a calf. She was Polly's project every year until she was too old for 4-H. When Polly was older, she worked as a counselor at 4-H camp every year. It got to where every 4-H kid in the county knew Fancy.

On the first day of the fair on Labor Day weekend, there was always a steady stream of kids coming to the Dairy Barn to check on Fancy. Fancy seemed to enjoy the attention. They used to put a big banner over her back advertising the 4-H milkshake booth and parade her around the fairgrounds. Again, Fancy seemed to enjoy it.

After six years of shows, when my sister became too old to be in 4-H, Fancy's fair career was over. That summer when we were getting our show string ready, Fancy stood by the gate the whole time, beckoning to us to take her along. She knew it was "fair time" and was expecting to go.

My sister went off to college that fall, and during the winter of 1978 we found Fancy dead in her stall one morning. I've always wondered if Fancy died of a broken heart.

Terrell Timmons is a lifelong farmer living in Ashland County, Ohio. His family raises mostly corn and alfalfa, and they have Holstein cattle. His two children, Megan and Ian, are involved with 4-H and their local FFA chapter.

Halter Breaking "CC"

Cathy Thomas

I was getting increasingly concerned as the cute spring calf gained more and more weight, aging into a yearling heifer. I was waiting for my brother, Don, to halter break the heifer for his daughter Airyn, future heifer "showman."

It was a beautiful spring day when I decided that I would take charge of halter breaking this potential show heifer and get her to a point that my 10-year-old niece could handle. By this point in time, that cute little Black Angus, named "CC" for "Cute Cow," weighed over 500 pounds and was as strong-headed as they come.

I decided that the best bet was to get a halter on the beast and tie her off to a post for short periods of time, until she stopped fighting the pressure. After a few days of "post work," CC would just stand there, bracing herself, waiting for me to try and outweigh her! I considered myself to be a seasoned farmhand, having shown beef, dairy, and sheep on Maine's Agricultural Fair Circuit for over 10 years. And after weighing my options, I decided that a truck with a Reese hitch would do quite nicely for continuing with the training!

At the outset it seemed like a wonderfully easy idea. After all, if CC pulled back, she'd only harm herself and stop pulling - - right?

It started out going very well. I had a helper in the back of the truck to guide me on the appropriate speed, telling me when the rope was taut or getting too loose. Everything was going very well. But rather than end on an easy note, why not try for just a little more? What could it hurt? So after "walking" CC down the hill about an eighth of a mile, I decided to "walk" her back up the hill!

At just about the time we reached the crest of the hill, the whole idea suddenly seemed rather foolish! CC got tired of walking, braced her legs, and then stopped walking. That, along with a sudden jerk of her head, left her breathless – literally!

She backed up quickly, leaving the rope halter so tight on her head that I couldn't see it through the fat on her face. CC stood there for a moment, then dropped to her knees, and then went flat out on her side with her legs straight out! I could not believe it!

All sorts of thoughts went through my head. "Once a cow is down, that's it; they have given up and will die." And what would I tell my niece? "Airyn, sorry to tell you this but I killed your little 'Cute Cow.'" "Don, I'm not quite sure what to say, but your first born-and-bred animal is dead and tied to the back of my truck!"

About that time, her legs started to stiffen, and I knew that I might as well tie myself to the truck and go down with her!

I yelled at my helper to go to the barn and get a knife or a scissors, and she came back with a sickle blade! Although tempted, I decided to not "end it there" and got the rope halter off of CC. When the strain of the halter was off, a small pool of blood drained from the heifer's nose and onto the ground.

In a panic, I began to roll the heifer. She didn't do much and her legs were out stiff, leaving only a few inches of space in which to roll her back and forth. I considered mouth-to-mouth resuscitation. But in total frustration, I jumped on CC's belly a few times, rolled her, and then jumped on her again!

I was leaning against her, trying to think up a good story to tell Don and Airyn, when CC coughed, spit up a little more blood, and suddenly jumped up to her feet! I couldn't believe it! She was standing and breathing - - two very good signs!

After a vet check, some extensive explaining, and a promise not to halter break any more heifers, I am now allowed back in the barn to feed and pat the animals only! "CC" lived, went on to become a beautiful show heifer, and led like a "pro" after her life-altering experience!

Cathy Thomas is the leader of the Fresh Horse's 4-H club in Pittston, Maine. She is the owner of a small, family-run business that jacks and moves buildings, and owns 10 horses, two dogs, and a pot-bellied pig. She has one child, but her home is open to all children of all ages, all of the time!

Bovine Drama

"Tew milk a kicking cow, stand oph about 10 foot,
and holler 'So! darn you.'"

Josh Billings (1818 - 1885)
American humorist and lecturer, author of *Old Farmer's
Allminax*

"Ferdy"
Tiffany McMillan

I grew up in the country outside of Austin, Texas, in the town of Spicewood, on eight and a half acres of land. We had a favorite bull called Ferdinand, or "Ferdy" for short. His female mate was named "Spook." She was scared of everyone and everything, totally the opposite of our friendly bull. Ferdy loved to be petted, scratched, and made to be the center of attention. He seemed very large, at over 1,500 pounds, as I was a tall, lanky 13-year old when this story took place.

My dad liked to call the cows to us and show us how to give them attention. He was very proud of how he had tamed the bull and tried for as long as I can remember to also tame the mother and the babies so they would come to him as well.

Ferdy and Spook had several babies over the years. The calves were always the best part of farm life for me. I used to get down on my hands and knees in the pasture and crawl to the growing calves. Everyone thought I was crazy! All of our family photo albums contain pictures of me and the cows "kissing," although it was really just my nose touching their wet, snotty noses. It was so much fun for me to get so close to the babies. And that was something my dad couldn't or wouldn't do. He had a way with his bull, and I, with the babies.

We never kept the babies after weaning them from "Spook." It was hard for me to say "goodbye" to them, but that was always part of the deal.

Over the years our cows became an attraction for our neighbors. They liked to come over for barbecues, and they would try to pet Ferdy. My dad would give the neighbors lessons on how to befriend our bull and how to handle him like he did. My dad is a big fellow, so he could let Ferdy rub and bump up against his hip without it really fazing him. However, if anyone else had attempted that, they probably would have been injured.

I think Ferdy had a certain amount of respect for my dad. He would get the cows some pellets or feed cubes and put them in a five-gallon bucket. Dad would stand in the grass a good distance from the house, shaking the bucket and saying, "SOOOO….COW!," in a really high-pitched voice. The sound of the cubes hitting that bucket would have them running in no time. (Cows aren't fast runners, but they never moved faster than when it was time for feed.)

One particular day I tried to feed those big, hungry animals the way my daddy had shown me. I put the feed cubes in the bucket, just like he told me to. I had our neighbors as my audience, as well as my brother, sister, dad, and stepmom.

Back behind our house was a shed with a fenced-in area for confining the cows when the pasture was mowed. (That's the only time the cattle ever saw this area.) Needless to say,

I didn't see it much either, but I always knew it was there. It was fenced with thick chicken wire about six feet high - - just a little temporary holding pen.

Now let's get back to the cubes. I had the bucket ready to go. This was my first attempt at my dad's bucket-feeding technique. I was excited and scared at the same time, as these cows were much bigger than I, and they were not my pets. I knew they'd be running as soon as they heard those cubes.

Daddy told me to shake the bucket. I started shaking that bucket and yelling "SOOOO.... COW!!" In a matter of seconds, there was a full-grown heifer, a 1500-pound bull (complete with horns), and a large calf running straight at me.

I froze for a moment. My dad hadn't prepared me for the fear I was experiencing. I thought I was going to have a heart attack in the process of being trampled down by these beasts! I was so small and thin, and they all looked so big, and all I could think of was how they were coming straight for me, and fast!

My next instinct was to run...so off I went. I led those cows all over the eight and a half acres, scared to death that I was about to "meet my maker." The farther I ran, the farther they chased me. They wouldn't give up! I was soon running out of energy, and the bucket was getting heavier and heavier with my every running step. All I could hear was everyone laughing as they watched me "run for my life," trying to escape a trio of the friendliest cattle in existence.

I began to panic and couldn't catch my breath. I couldn't lose the cattle, and I was running out of options.

I finally remembered the corral back behind the house. I ran to it, still dragging the bucket of cubes, and went to one of the corners. I'm not sure if I had run out of other options or what I was thinking! The three cows followed me into the corral and came straight at me. At that moment, I thought I was going to be gored by the bull!

Ferdy came right at me, with horns swinging wildly, as he attempted to get closer and closer. My audience was no longer visible at this point. I was alone and scared to death. I scaled that chicken wire fence backward, clinging to the bucket, until there was no more fence to climb, and I screamed for my daddy as loud as I could.

He hollered back at me, "Dump the bucket out, goofy!"

I turned that bucket upside down and watched as all of the cows' attention went from skinny little me to the treats on the ground, and the cattle went crazy, trying to eat those cubes as fast as they could. That was my chance to escape! I was crying hysterically, and I couldn't breathe.

If only I had foreseen the outcome of trying to be just like my dad, with his cow-feeding "show," I would never have tried that! I never attempted to do anything "special" like that again with the cows, except to "kiss" the babies, after that frightening incident!

Tiffany McMillan hails from Austin, Texas, and prides herself on being far from ordinary. As a young, single mother of two young children, she believes that writing is the best medicine for EVERYTHING. Her years in Spicewood, Midland, and Austin have provided her with a lifetime of rich western imagery, and she lives in a region and time in which rough-riding, lasso-twirling, and cattle drives are not just the ways of the past.

The Bull . . . and I

Roger Stoner

I grew up in the '60s in a small town in northwest Iowa. Back in those days, town kids were a steady source of labor for area farmers. I started working for several farmers when I was in my early teens, and by the time I completed my sophomore year of high school, my brother-in-law offered me steady work on his farm for the entire summer. I lived on his farm that summer and learned how to operate farm machinery, as well as how to do the livestock chores, including milking the cows.

By the end of the following summer, I considered myself an old hand on the farm. So I didn't hesitate when my brother-in-law asked me if I could do chores by myself for four days after school had started that fall. He and my sister were going to a "Young Farmers" seminar in Chicago and needed someone to milk the cows.

Chores on the weekend were done on the regular schedule, but the weekdays presented a problem for me. I had football practice, which meant that the cows would have to get milked about an hour and a half earlier and an hour and a half later than usual on weekdays. The schedule change was no big deal to me, but as it turned out, it was a big deal to the cows.

The cow yard had a muddy pool stretching from one fence line to the other, making it necessary for the cows to wade through a quagmire of mud and water before entering the milking barn. To provide a clean, dry place for the cows to bed down at night, my brother-in-law had dumped several loads of corncobs in a large pile in the highest area in the cow yard.

The weekend schedule change went fine, although by the time for the evening milking, the cows were uncomfortable and very anxious to be milked. But on Monday I would have to milk the cows at 4:00 a.m. in order to make sure I could make it to school on time.

That morning I got up at 3:30 a.m. I dressed in my barn clothes, pulled on my knee-high milking boots, and donned a warm jean jacket before facing the frosty cold and early morning darkness. I went to the barn, turned on the lights, and flipped on the radio. After dispensing a small pile of ground corn feed in front of each stanchion, I opened the barn door and called for the cows.

"Heeer boss, boss, bossy – heeer boss, boss, bossy," I hollered into the darkness.

It usually just took the sound of my voice and the smell of the feed, the light from the barn and the sound of my favorite radio station to get their attention, but not that muddy morning. It had been only about seven hours since the cows had been milked the night before. Another hour and a half and they'd probably be running, but I didn't have time to wait. It was clear that they weren't coming in on their own. I had to get things going, or I was going to be late for school.

I walked out into the cow yard, wading through the shallow end of the muddy pool and up onto the corn cob pile, where I started kicking the cows out of their cozy dry beds. It was dark, and I was in a hurry, when I made the mistake of kicking the Bull in the rump and shouting at him to get up!

He was a purebred Holstein that my brother-in-law kept to breed his milk cows. Just shy of six feet tall at the shoulder and nearly seven feet long, he was a massive animal, tipping the scales at 1,998 pounds, only two pounds short of a ton!

Dairy breed bulls have a long reputation of being difficult and aggressive, if not just plain ornery and downright mean. But for the most part, this Bull had shown very few of those tendencies. Oh, he eyeballed you when you walked through the cow yard and stood his ground if you walked toward him when driving the cows from one pen to another. But he always chose to follow the cows, rather than lead them at your urging.

When I kicked the Bull, instead of the usual slow motion – easing hind end up first, followed by the pushing up of the front legs, like the way the cows stand up – the Bull leaped to his feet like a cat - - a 2,000-pound cat! Then he spun around and stood there, near the top of the cob pile, facing downward, eyes locked in a stare-down with me. He bellowed in anger, and I could feel his hot breath on my suddenly cold, pale face. This was not a good situation!

I took a tentative step backward, and he took a confident step forward. I took another step, and so did he. I was too scared to turn my back and run, figuring that if I did, he would simply run me down and trample me. What light remained from the slowly fading stars shone off his docked horns, and his eyes were glowing with anger. He followed me down the cob pile, staying close to me, pausing occasionally to snort, bellow, and throw his head from side to side, and pitching dirt back over his shoulder with his slimy snout.

I continued in my slow retreat, backing away, and noticed that I was gaining some separation from him as he stood pawing the dirt. And a little too late, I realized that I had managed to back myself into the middle of the deepest, muddiest part of the quagmire.

The Bull's agitation grew as I backed even farther into the muddy pool. At about the moment that I thought I could make a run for the fence, I noticed that the cold water from the quagmire was pouring over my boot tops, and that my feet were stuck firmly in the mud. There was no turning to run away now! I would have to face this thing to the bitter end!

Suddenly, the Bull charged! My only escape plan was to fall into the mud one way or the other and hope that his momentum would carry him over and past me! As he lunged toward me, I tensed, ready to make my muddy life-saving flop.

But when his front feet splashed into the cold water, he skidded to a halt, splashing mud all over me! Then he turned his back and walked calmly back up onto the dry cob pile, where he casually lay back down. In disbelief, I wondered if by not turning and running I had called his bluff, or if he just didn't want to get his hooves wet.

Still shaking with fear and anger, I stepped out of my mud-stuck boots and went up to the house. Grabbing my 12-gauge shotgun and mumbling something about making 1,998 pounds of hamburger, I stomped back into the cow yard and drove the cows into the barn for milking. And the Bull, apparently satisfied with giving me the worst scare of my life, didn't even look in my direction.

Roger Stoner published *The Peterson Patriot* (Peterson, Iowa) for over 15 years, doing a lot of the writing, including his weekly column, "Roger's Remarks." He and his wife have two grown children and six wonderful grandchildren. He's been published in magazines, and the novel he wrote is looking for an agent or publisher. He works for Eaton Corporation of Spencer, Iowa, and enjoys hunting, fishing, woodworking, and wood carving.

Saving Polly's Life

Robert Stewart

It was June of 1948. I guess I might have been about nine years old. Dad was a tenant on a rented farm where we milked about 18 cows.

The family was gone somewhere that day, and for some reason some of us kids were left home alone. I was playing around the barn that lazy afternoon, when I saw Polly in the barnyard having trouble. Even at that young age, I recognized that she was bloated. Her sides protruded like she had six calves inside her! I figured she had gotten into the alfalfa field and couldn't stop eating. I sensed she needed help real quick.

What was a nine-year-old boy to do? There were no cell phones in those days and no close neighbors to call. I wasn't yet aware that I could call the veterinarian. Polly was foaming at the mouth.

Something told me to start chasing her. It was all I could think to do. At first Polly wasn't too keen about going anywhere. I could see that she was hurting inside, making me all the more determined to get her on the run.

So around and around that barnyard we went. Barefooted me in hot pursuit, swatting the old gal on the rump with a stick every time she slowed down! In a short while,

"BUUUUUUUUUUUUURP!" Then another, "BUUUUU-UUUUUUUURP," and then another and another, until finally there were no burps coming from Polly and her sides no longer protruded.

I found out many years later that my solution was certainly not the right treatment for bloat. To this day I don't know what made me decide to chase her, and I don't remember what Dad said about it when he came home. All I remember is the relief that the old cow got from all of those humongous belches and the satisfaction that I got from probably saving her life.

Robert Stewart is a 69-year-old crop farmer whose love for agriculture helped him survive two bouts of cancer. He is a licensed pyrotechnic and restores a fleet of antique tractors. Robert has been married for 44 years and has four children and eight grandchildren.

Bull-headed Bull

Chuck G. Hosford

Sometime in the early 1950s, my father purchased a short-horned bull named "Barney" for our farm. When we bought him, Barney was too stubborn to be loaded into a truck. After a few hours, the men only succeeded in tying one end of a long rope around the bull's horns. My father struggled for hours to lead him to a pasture on the west side of our farm.

Barney first took my father about a mile down the gravel road toward the highway, then back up another road leading past the east side of our farm. He refused to go up our driveway and continued another two miles up the road. After dragging my father up and down the road for another hour or so, the nearly half-ton creature finally went up our driveway and into the barnyard. After this difficult delivery, I was warned to stay away from this dangerous animal.

A couple of weeks later, on a very hot summer afternoon, I was cleaning out the horse barn. I scooped up a pitchfork of stinky, dirty straw and threw it out the doorway and into the barnyard. A moment later, Barney entered the barn. His powerful legs easily carried his sturdy body over the threshold. I shouted, "Get out!" in my loudest and angriest voice, but he glared at me with penetrating eyes and kept lunging closer.

He stopped and pawed the dirty floor, flexed his slimy nostrils, and snorted angrily. Barney continued pawing the floor, then suddenly lowered his head and closed his eyes. I had watched enough cartoons in my lifetime that I could visualize the next scene. And I never could stand the sight of blood, especially when it was mine.

Suddenly, he charged, and I panicked. I froze and closed my eyes, expecting my life to end in a brief and painful moment. Then I heard a loud, barn-shaking thud, as if something hit a solid object. I opened my eyes and saw Barney down on his front knees, with his head against a massive oak mainstay that held the barn upright. I couldn't believe he missed me! The bull shook his head, stood up, and briefly looked at me. Then he raced out of the barn.

After that incident I could make Barney do almost anything I wanted. My father apparently noticed that the half-ton beast and I were like old friends, because a few days later he put his arm around my shoulders and told me that Barney had been going over the south fence, and that our neighbor was threatening to shoot him the next time.

I was no dummy. I knew my half-ton buddy was flirting with the neighbor's frisky Hereford heifer. Father gave me permission to forget about all my other chores for a day and sent me out to the pasture to stand watch on the bull.

When I stepped into the pasture, Barney was eating the grass and generally behaving himself. I found a place to sit in the shade and relax. At lunchtime, one of my sisters brought me a ham sandwich and a thermos of ice water. I was about to take a bite of my sandwich when Barney abruptly turned and gazed toward the south fence. I knew what would happen next, but I hoped it wouldn't. He started off, trotting proudly with a purpose, toward the south fence. If I couldn't stop him before he crossed into the neighbor's property, his life could be cut short with a "bang," and I would disappoint my father.

I raced for the south fence, dropping my sandwich. Fortunately, I was a fast runner back then. I put both hands on the fence and propelled my lean body over it without missing a step. Barney raced up the next hill. It was level ground on our neighbor's side of the fence, which gave me an advantage. I ran parallel to the bull, watching closely as he charged up the hill.

I stopped to take a breath and looked up at the steep incline. At that point, Barney was stomping on the woven wire fence with his immense weight. I waved my arms wildly and yelled, with no one but the bull and the heifer to hear me. (If I had known then what goes on in a bull's mind when pursuing a "romantic interest," I would never have stood in his path!) I continued for several minutes, trying to get Barney's attention with my ungainly teen antics.

Finally, Barney stopped his fence-stomping efforts to stare at me. We both "froze" for a moment. His interest in the opposite gender may have been overridden by his fear of another serious dull headache. He turned around and trotted back into the lush pasture.

I managed to keep Barney "at bay" in this manner for several long, hot summer days. I guess I "saved Barney's life" for awhile, and I got an early start on my writing career, with all of those quiet hours in the shade in that pasture. And I think Barney never forgot who gave him that terrible headache, at least while I lived on the farm.

Chuck G. Hosford lived in the Council Bluffs, Iowa, area before graduating from high school. His careers have included: electronics technician, software engineer, and technical writer. While serving in the U.S. Navy, he visited several islands in the Pacific Ocean. Upon retirement, he became a fiction writer, weaving past travels into his first novel, *Time Warp to Hong Kong*, published in 2008.

Bovine Protection Squad

Sheila Paquet

I'll admit to not being very closely involved in the day-to-day operation of our family dairy farm while I was growing up. I was even less involved once I went off to college, began a career, and established my own single-girl apartment. However, I always thought of the farm as "going home," and the cows were a constant part of the landscape, their daily lives not known to be full of excitement.

One year I went home for Father's Day weekend. I was in the house alone, preparing a nice Father's Day meal for my dad, who was out in the barn doing the evening chores. My mom had run to the store. The doorbell chimed as I was taking a pan of cookies out of the oven. Still acting like I lived there, I opened the door to admit two uniformed police officers into the kitchen. (This was not an everyday occurrence by any means!)

The lead officer pointed out the kitchen window overlooking the pasture and asked, "Are those your cows?" I responded that the cows in question did indeed belong to the farm. The officer continued, "We were just driving by, and we think one of them may be hurt."

At this point, we moved the conversation outside, so as to get a clearer view of the pasture. I asked him how they drew this conclusion and if they could point out the injured animal.

Both officers gazed intently at the pasture, and the one who began the conversation confidently reported, "It's that one, the white one with the black spots." (I should point out that it was a pasture full of Holsteins, and while the size of their spots varies, they all have black spots.)

It seemed that the lead officer was going to do all of the talking. "Well, we noticed that it's lying on its side..." (For some reason, I thought it prudent to interrupt a police officer to assure him that all of the animals in the pasture were indeed cows, therefore he could safely say "she" instead of "it.") The officer pressed on, with a brick red blush creeping up his neck, "She was lying on her side and all of the other cows seemed to be gathered around its...er, her...um...butt... area...," he struggled to finish. Then he soldiered on and added, "They all seemed concerned about her."

By now I was choking on my laughter, because between his description and what I could clearly see happening in the pasture, we'd obviously just welcomed a new calf to the farm!

Both officers appeared greatly relieved to see that the object of their concern was back on her feet. They dusted off their hands as if finishing up a job well done and wished me a good evening.

I think I managed to thank them for their concern without laughing too hard, but as soon as their cruiser peeled out of the driveway, I wasted no time in running to the barn to report to my dad that the local police had added "overseeing bovine births" to their list of duties.

Sheila Paquet was born and raised on a Wisconsin dairy farm, where a runaway cow once tried to join her seventh birthday party. After surviving other assorted bovine antics through the years, she grew up to be a freelance marketing writer who still lives and works in the middle of America's Dairy State.

"Hunter"

Helen Meadows

That Wednesday morning, six days into calving season, Bill, Helen, and their son, Jake, walked through the ankle-deep snow to the clearing where Rose waited with her new calf. Bill carried the scale and ear tags, focused on his ranching job of identifying and weighing each new addition to the herd.

"Watch out, Mom, don't get too close. Sometimes Rose can be a little testy after she's calved," Jake warned his mother.

Helen advanced cautiously, and let out a gasp of surprise. "Look at her!"

The calf, flanked by her mother, was a striking red. Her face was white, except for the twin patches around each eye, the goggles Bill favored. A white band circled each of her hind legs. A thick, uneven brown streak appeared to be the work of a child who had taken a burnt umber crayon and scribbled where her mouth was supposed to be, turning the ends up into a smile.

"Isn't that funny? She has such a comical look about her!" Helen exclaimed.

Bill wanted to call her "Red-Eyed Rosie" after her father, "Red-Eyed Jack," and mother, "Rose," but Helen wanted the name to be "Rose Crayon" because of her fascinating features. "It looks like Renita colored her mouth with a crayon."

(Renita, their grown-up daughter, asked, "Why did you say I colored her mouth? Why me?" And I told her, "Because you're the one who always loved the cows, that's why.")

In the end, they each called her what they wanted. When Bill spoke of her, it was "Red-Eyed Rosie."

"You mean 'Rose Crayon,'" Helen would correct. Whatever the name, she had a nature as sweet as clover, loving to be scratched and petted. While most of the calves would curiously step forward for a bit to look and sniff, they would scatter if a person got close enough to actually touch them. But Rose Crayon stood and enjoyed the attention and the petting. In fact, she went so far as to lay her head right on Bill's shoulder, looking for all the world as if she intended to waltz with him, although the only things moving were his fingers, as he scratched them up and down her neck.

"She sure is tame. Wouldn't it be nice if all of our cattle were as gentle as she is?" Helen mused.

Rose Crayon grew and developed into a beautiful heifer. Soon she was heavy with calf, and the couple waited for calving season to begin.

One particularly chilly March, Bill went on a business trip for a couple of nights. "Be sure to check the cattle each night, and see if any are due to calve." He went on, "There's a couple that are pretty close."

"Of course, I'll do all that I can," Helen assured him.

By the end of the week, no new additions had appeared. Helen did the chores before supper and checked the cattle once more. Finding no cow in labor, she went into the house where there was a cozy fire.

Bill arrived at the ranch as the clock was nearing 11:00 p.m. Early the following morning, muffled against the winter weather, he went out to check the cows. The only sound was the horn of a distant train, carrying for miles on the still air. After his eyes adjusted to the shadows, he noticed a dark form in the pines on a hill. Rose Crayon was standing off by herself. Bill took a step forward and his stomach lurched. Rose Crayon had calved, but the sac still covered the newborn calf's nose and had caused it to suffocate. The new mother stood over her motionless baby, waiting for it to move.

The situation seemed to call for quiet. Bill scratched Rose Crayon's forehead. His breath was visible in small clouds as he talked. "Shoot. You would have made a good mother."

A short time later, Bill remarked to Helen, "I'm going to milk Rose Crayon in case we need a nurse cow. I'll put her in the corral."

Rose Crayon adapted to milking in an affable manner. Her tail didn't swish and sting his face, and her cloven hooves didn't strike him. As Bill crouched, one knee on the ground, her leg lifted a few inches in the air. The milk continued streaming into the metal bowl as the leg made a gentle arc before setting back down.

"I think Red-Eyed Rosie likes to be played with. She doesn't kick, just swings that ole leg out," Bill said, with an amused tone in his voice as he stepped into the kitchen carrying a bowl of warm milk. He milked the cows twice a day. The cream was used in the topping for strawberry shortcake, whipped into a delicate pale yellow butter, or fed as a treat to Sal, the farm dog, and all of the barn cats.

The weather moderated, and the calendar page was turned to April. Bill and Sal made their daily rounds among the herd, admiring the frolicking calves and checking for any new arrivals.

In the cool dimness of the ancient tall pines, Durham, a muscular brindle cow, was industriously licking a wobbly-legged newborn. Tan and dark irregular flecks decorated the face of the newly arrived creature.

"Man, if she isn't a miniature version of her mother," Bill murmured. "Has the same brindle markings as her mother. She even kinda looks like that candy bar. Guess I'll call her 'Lil Snicker.'" He could almost see the pride in Durham's face as she diligently cleaned off her offspring.

Sal was investigating ahead, following her nose, a full hundred yards away. The dog paused, ears erect, feathery tail sweeping the ground at what she found. Bill straightened up; the ground made a soft crunch-crunch sound under his leather boots as he covered the distance to the dog. One glance confirmed his suspicions; a second calf, shiny-wet from birth, lay curled up in a pod of long-stemmed grass.

"Good dog, Sal! Good girl for finding the calf," Bill praised. With long strides, he circled back around Durham, pushing her toward the discovery. As the cow moved closer, disinterest was written all over her face. The calf, a beautiful nutmeg color, struggled to its feet and tried to walk to Durham. Jerking her head, Durham ignored this calf, which was only one shade of brown, lacking the unique markings of the other twin.

The cow bowed out. Ducking out of Bill's reach, and nosing against "Lil Snicker," Durham whisked her favored twin calf toward the far reaches of the meadow. She didn't even cast a backward glance at the calf in the "plain brown wrapper," which was desperately attempting to follow her.

"Stupid cow! She abandoned it without even licking it off or letting it nurse," Bill grumbled to his furry companion. Letting out an exasperated sigh, he turned toward the house. Opening the door to the mudroom, he hollered, "Need help! Durham calved awhile ago. She had twins and claimed just one. Will you keep an eye on the other one while I get the tractor?"

Stationing himself just inside the round pen, Bill opened the gate and called Rose Crayon. After she stepped into the enclosure, he scratched her head with the tips of his fingers and murmured, "Good girl." As much as he loved ranching, he hated it when calving didn't go as Mother Nature intended, and he had to step in to graft a neglected calf onto an unrelated cow. The challenge was especially difficult, even with his entire "bag of tricks." The Nutri-drench, frozen colostrum, and esophageal tubing apparatus made it a little easier. Sometimes the cow wanted nothing to do with another cow's calf and would kick at anything within reach. The odds of the abandoned calf's survival were looking more dismal with each passing minute. This twin hadn't nursed at all yet and would undoubtedly be very weak. He drew a deep breath and focused on the job at hand, dreading the chaos that lay ahead.

Five minutes later they walked to where the calf was lying. Lifting it to its feet, they began walking toward the shallow hollow. Bill left to get the tractor while Helen waited at the edge of the pine trees. A minute ticked by. Watching the tiny heifer, a wave of pity flooded her heart.

The forgotten calf tried to follow a horned cow that was ambling along the dusty cow path. But that cow didn't want anything to do with another cow's baby. Lowering her head and butting the calf aside, she continued down the path until she was out of sight.

Hoping for a more favorable reception, the calf spied a dark red cow approaching. The cow eyed her with suspicion before shooing her out of the way.

The calf paused, as if it knew its destination, and headed down the grassy slope. The next encounter was with a steer calf that came up to sniff, investigate, and perhaps to play. But the abandoned, nameless calf did not want to play. The calf seemed to think that the steer might be her mother, nosing at the steer's hind legs in search of milk. Startled, the steer backed up in surprise and bounded away.

Not surprisingly, the calf wandered up on long spindly legs to Helen, lowered her head, and nosed Helen's blue jeans. Running a hand across the calf's face, Helen laughed. "Whoa! I'm not your mother. Come on, let's go over by the fence." Gripping the calf and scooting along, she guided the weak calf forward.

Climbing onto his tractor, Bill reached for the ignition, and sat for a moment with the door open and the engine running, working out a plan. He resigned himself to spending the rest of the afternoon trying to teach a heifer to adopt another cow's calf. He steered the lumbering machine through the pasture gate to where Helen waited with the solid-colored calf.

"This wasn't built for comfort, but it's faster than walking," Helen said, as they hoisted what seemed to be all legs into the tractor's bucket.

"Poor little thing. She's having a hard time. You should have seen her searching. We should name her 'Hunter' because she's hunting for her mother."

"And she doesn't have one yet," Bill replied, "and probably never will."

Neither of them spoke for awhile.

"Well, we've got to try, anyway," Helen urged.

Helen took her position next to the tractor bucket. Step by step, one arm holding the calf in the makeshift "cage," she kept pace with the tractor as Bill slowly moved across the pasture. With a happy tail slicing the air, Sal merrily ran alongside.

A short while later, the couple lifted the newborn calf out of the tractor's bucket and scooted it into the round pen.

"Don't get your hopes up. It's been two weeks since Red-Eyed Rosie lost her calf. I'd be real surprised if she took to this one," Bill remarked as he turned and headed for the house. "I hope we can save it."

The late afternoon sunlight spread across the area where Bill had forked some hay into a pile. Bending over, Helen scooped up an armful of the grass hay. Spreading it in front of Rose Crayon, she quietly said, "I'm going to pull a fast one on you." With a quick swipe of her hand, Helen brushed some strands of grass from Rose Crayon's coat and nudged the calf in the direction of the heifer. "Here's your new baby, Crayon!"

Rose Crayon cocked her head, looked at Helen, and if she could have spoken English, may have inquired, "Where did you find that?"

Hunter didn't waste a second. In the few hours of her lifetime, she knew what to do. Her hooves raised tiny circles of dust in the pen as she moved to Rose Crayon's side.

Bill momentarily stalled in his tracks, supplies cradled in his arms. The metal handle of the bucket was cool beneath his palms as his senses were filled with the scene unfolding before his very eyes. Rose Crayon's head was bent over, munching hay. She stood chewing and swallowing, strands of hay dangling like freshly cooked spaghetti noodles out of the corners of her mouth. Hunter's backside was pointed in Bill's direction, tail a-swishing like a pendulum; her head was buried into Rose Crayon's udder, and as she was nursing, a frothy white slobber dripped down her chin.

They made a beautiful pair that spring day, a tawny newborn's coat snuggled against the rich mahogany-colored one of a newly found adoptive mother.

A light breeze carried the sweet aroma of hay. Bill's breath came in gasps as he took in the full drama of what had just happened. He set his calf-rescue "bag of tricks" aside.

Helen was taking it all in: the expression of disbelief, astonishment, and joy on Bill's face. And a big grin beamed across hers.

Helen Meadows is a native Montanan and grew up on a farm near Corvallis, Montana. She graduated from Montana State University with a B.S. in Home Economics, and volunteered for over 25 years as 4-H leader and culinary judge at the County Fair. Helen and her family currently raise Simmental/Red Angus cattle on their ranch in Sanders County, Montana.

Dairy Princesses

"Now when anyone says 'Say cheese!,'
I always think 'crumbles.'"

Jennifer Fieber Zirbel
*1997 South Dakota Dairy Princess and inventor
of Kraft Cheese Crumbles*

About Dairy Princesses of the U.S....

In many states in the U.S., it is an annual tradition to crown a state-level dairy princess as well as county-level dairy princesses. The young women receiving the highest awards are crowned before or during their State Fairs. They all must be connected to the dairy industry through living on dairy farms or by employment on dairy farms.

The dairy princesses are goodwill ambassadors for their state's dairy industry and make many media appearances throughout the year of their reign. They also visit schools, fairgrounds, and consumer events and are knowledgeable about the dairy industry. All of them inform the public, especially children, about the health benefits of delicious and nutritious dairy products.

Many of the dairy princess programs are in the Midwest, where there is still an abundance of family-owned dairy farms. The North Dakota Dairy Princess Program is the longest-running program in the U.S. Some of the other states with programs are Virginia, South Dakota, Pennsylvania, Iowa, and Minnesota.

Minnesota's contest is called the *Princess Kay of the Milky Way*. The name "Princess Kay of the Milky Way" was chosen from over 10,000 names suggested in a 1954 contest to name the Minnesota princess. "Butterhead" sculptures of the newly crowned *Princess Kay of the Milky Way,* the state-level princess, and 11 other princesses are carved in 90-pound blocks of butter, one per day, in a large, glassed-in, refrigerated sculpting booth at the Minnesota State Fair. The revolving yellow butter sculptures are world-renowned.

The Midwest Dairy Association sponsors the Princess Kay of the Milky Way program with funds provided by dairy farmers. The Midwest Dairy Association is a non-profit organization that provides consumers with information about the nutrition and wholesomeness of dairy foods and conducts research and promotional programs.

Eleanor Maley with cheese samples in 1954.
Photo courtesy of Midwest Dairy Association.

The First Princess Kay of the Milky Way

Eleanor Maley Thatcher

Princess Kay of the Milky Way, 1954

One spring day, my 4-H leader informed me that she had entered my name in the competition for the first-ever good-will ambassador for the Minnesota dairy industry. I had just been the "queen's attendant" for advanced sewing at the state-level 4-H competition, so I had a stylish dress all ready to go for the first round of the contest.

There was a lot of enthusiasm for the 1954 pageant, with 2800 girls in Minnesota entering their county's competitions. Candidates were judged on poise, personality, exuberance, speaking ability, and a pleasing appearance, vying for this healthy role model position for the dairy industry. The winner from each of 15 regions went on to the contest at the State Fair. In that regional competition, at the age of 17, I was crowned the Mower County Dairy Princess.

Shortly thereafter, I was on the stage in front of thousands at the Minnesota State Fair. Governor Orville Lothrop Freeman was on the stage. The princess contestants were each driven around the arena, with escorts, in convertibles. Once onstage, U.S. Navy cadets stood at attention in their dress whites. The crowd cheered as the 2nd and 1st runners-up were chosen. When I heard the words, "And our first Princess

Kay of the Milky Way is......Eleanor Maley of Grand Meadow," it was an absolutely breathtaking moment, which I will never forget.

Following my coronation, I did a lot of traveling, logging about 250,000 miles that year. Princess Kay became my "full time job"; being a high school student was on the side, but I still managed to graduate as salutatorian of my class. I was also named as the first National Dairy Princess for the American Dairy Association in October of 1954.

One of my duties as Princess Kay was to crown other dairy princesses. I crowned the North and South Dakota dairy princesses that year. I handed out cheese and milk samples almost everywhere I went, at supermarkets and county fairs, and always wearing a big smile! Cow-milking contests were also part of the job, so it's a good thing I was competent at that as well.

In the month of June, which is "Dairy Month" in the Midwest, I made 45 appearances. I was constantly going from coronations to parades, to meetings and photo opportunities, and appearing with major political figures like Senator Hubert H. Humphrey, Senator Edward J. Thye, and Lyndon B. Johnson (prior to his vice presidency).

I became a "quick change artist," sometimes changing from my drum majorette costume after a local Grand Meadow parade, into a stiff metal-hoop-skirted evening gown, as modestly as possible in the back of a flashy loaned baby-blue

Cadillac. As the first Princess Kay, and doing double-duty as the National Dairy Princess, I always had to be ready to go "on stage" as America's dairy industry ambassador. So the day after Christmas, off I went to Paris.

My experience in France was a huge contrast from my quiet life in the farming countryside of rural Minnesota. I presented 48 glass "quarter" bottles of milk, one from each of our then-48 states, to French Premier Mendes. The Premier was on a one-Frenchman dairy campaign, encouraging the Parisians to drink more milk than wine. (To my knowledge, they are still drinking wine with their cheese over there!) The paparazzi kept trying to hand me bottles of champagne, but I politely declined every time. I couldn't be pictured holding party-time champagne instead of healthful milk! I was the American dairy industry's role model, and I would not let my country down.

My title in France was "Miss Lait" (Miss Milk). News-reels in the U.S. and many countries, including Japan and Russia, ran footage of my France trip prior to the "feature film" in theatres. Movies like Hitchcock's *Rear Window* and the newly released *Seven Samurai* were preceded by images of this tiara-topped milky-white 17-year old, along with my pitch to drink a healthful glass of milk or a enjoy a tasty cube of cheese. There was a four-page spread, all about me and my dairy industry reign, in a Paris magazine.

I was an international celebrity that year, and even received a marriage proposal from a Frenchman in my farm-country Minnesota mailbox, addressed with only the words, "Miss Lait, USA." That proposal was one of many that year, including one from an American hog producer, with the post-script: "by the way, if you need fence posts, I can sell them to you cheap."

Among the many highlights of my princess year was co-hosting the International Dairy Show in Chicago, along with Miss Universe. The two of us rode around the arena each night, on parade in a convertible. I also had the special honor of presenting a "milk bucket" of butter to Vice President Richard Nixon's wife, Pat, who later went on to become our nation's First Lady. I was a guest of Edward R. Murrow, and I appeared on the "Today Show" with host Dave Garroway.

There was a six percent increase in U.S. milk consumption during my reign, and a rise in butter prices that resulted in a decline in government price supports. The butter sculptures weren't done yet when I was Princess Kay. I was sculpted in butter for the first time in 2003 at the Minnesota State Fair, for the 50th celebration of the Princess Kay competition.

It's hard to imagine what my life would have been like without my experience as Princess Kay of the Milky Way. It was an honor and a great adventure.

Eleanor Maley Thatcher went on to work as an audiologist for the State Hospital in Rochester, Minnesota. Her family has owned Thatcher Pools, Inc. in Rochester since 1967. She has three children and six grandchildren and leads a very active life, still playing tennis, skiing, and scuba diving.

Eleanor Maley Thatcher with her butterhead in August, 2003. © Richard Marshall, St. Paul Pioneer Press

The Butterhead Sculptor

Linda Christensen

Minnesota State Fair Butter Sculptor

I saw a television for the first time at the Minnesota State Fair. I believe I never missed a fair since then.

During one exceptionally hot and humid summer, I visited the fair building that housed dairy and animal product displays. There, inside a glass-sided cooler with a revolving floor, was a dairy princess in a snowsuit. An artist was carving a sculpture of her from an enormous solid block of butter. My companions and I marveled at the display and all agreed that we were envious of the two in that cold environment. I had an additional reason to want to be in that cooler: I dreamed of being an artist some day.

A few years later, in 1972, I graduated from art school and soon after received a call from the school, asking if I would be interested in doing the butter sculpture at the fair. Of course I said yes! In July I went to the fairgrounds and met a young woman who would be a model for me. I spent three hours in the cooler inside the dark and empty building, carving her sculptural portrait. I was hired before I finished.

The first day of the fair was the first time I actually carved an entire sculpture out of butter. When we walked into the cooler the first day, I saw the bright lights aimed at us and a great crowd of people looking in through the glass wall of the cooler, and I still wasn't certain I could finish a sculpture. If I made a bad mistake, I had no idea if I could even fix it. Suddenly I was frightened! But I did finish it, and I was proud of how beautiful the finished sculpture looked. When I was through with that first carving, I took off my gloves and used my bare, warm hands to smooth the surface. The pale yellow butter is translucent and soft looking, much prettier than the clay or plaster I had used until then.

I carve one dairy princess sculpture each day of the fair, for 12 consecutive days. Over the years, I have discovered that I can fix mistakes and repair accidents - - even if a sculpture falls on its face on the floor. I have learned a lot about cows and dairy farming, because all the princesses are part of the dairy industry, and we spend a whole day together and talk to one another most of the time. I like all of the attention I get for being one of the few people who do this fun and unusual job.

One of the most enjoyable things about what I do is hearing stories of what happens to the sculptures after the fair is over. The princesses all take their sculptures home insulated in layers of newspaper. Usually they put the sculptures in their freezers whole and later take them out again to tour around the county to different farm or county fair events. Some princesses use the sculptures at town corn-on-the-cob dinners and pancake breakfasts. Some have used their sculptures as centerpieces on their wedding tables. And other princesses have used the butter in cookies and baked goods to give as holiday presents. Many of the princesses come to the fair in later years and tell me they still have their sculpture; some even buy a special little freezer to keep it in. Many stories about the sculptures are printed in the newspaper or told on the TV news.

This year will be the 37th year I have done the butter sculpture. In Minnesota I'm known as "the lady who does the butterheads."

I would have been surprised, on that hot and humid day that I first saw the butter sculpture with my friends, to know that all of these years later I still have not missed a single state fair and that I would be such an amazing part of it.

Linda Christensen is a native Minnesotan who moved to California in 2003. She has two daughters and sons-in-law and six grandchildren in Minnesota. Between visiting her family and the fair, she spends some wonderful time every year in her beautiful home state.

Allison Benson butterhead, 2008. © John Hovland.

Who Inspired the Butter Carton Skirt?

For several years, **Mrs. John E. Miller**, a dairy farmer from Clara City, Minnesota, created milk and butter carton dresses for her daughter, **Jeanne**, to wear in the local Dairy Day Kiddie Parade.

Princess Kay saw the dress and was inspired to have one made to wear throughout her reign.

You have all seen that large photo of Karen Bracken, Princess Kay 1964. Her skirt was fashioned from 475 Minnesota butter cartons to call attention to the state's status as the #1 butter-producing state in the nation. A year later, Jeanne Miller, age 7, was summoned into town to have a photo taken with Karen… "and wear your butter carton dress, little Jeanne," she was told. Jeanne recalls being so excited to have her picture taken with Princess Kay… to help capture the inspiration for the now famous dress.

For 40 years **Jeanne Miller**, now **Jeanne Murphy**, has had a special fondness for the Princess Kay program. In fact, she is often there on the opening day of the fair to see who the new Princess Kay is. Jeanne Murphy of Montevideo and her husband, Mike, are with us here tonight. (please stand) We give Jeanne and her mom – **Iva** – thanks for being a special piece of the Princess Kay history.

Written for a Princess Kay banquet by Donna Moenning, Vice President, Industry Image & Relations for the Midwest Dairy Association, 2006.

Karen Bracken, Princess Kay of the Milky Way in 1964, wearing the butter carton skirt. The butter flaps from approximately 500 Minnesota creameries were used in creating the garment. Each flap was later returned to its creamery with a thank you note from Ms. Bracken. *Photo courtesy of Midwest Dairy Association.*

The North Dakota Dairy Queen of 1951

Shirley Ann (Brown) Gummer

The first Dairy Queen contest was held in 1947. North Dakota was the first state to hold such a contest.

In 1951, I was asked to compete for the title of North Dakota Dairy Queen. My sponsors were the North Dakota Brown Swiss Association and Harry Tonn, a Brown Swiss dairyman from Hillsboro, ND.

There were 22 girls, aged 16 to 22, competing for the title. I was the youngest. I entered the competition for a neat experience, thinking that I would never win. In fact, one of the older girls said to me, "Brownie, why don't you go home? You don't have a chance." I responded with, "I am here for the wonderful experience, thank you."

When you were a Dairy Queen contestant, you were required to sew a navy blue polka-dot dress, a little white apron, and a hat that resembled a Dutch bonnet. Now, my sewing left something to be desired, and my grandmother could certainly vouch for that! But I plowed through it and actually, the outfit did not look all that bad.

For the competition, each contestant had to perform a talent. I, along with five other girls, played the Norwegian Concerto. Not one of the piano solos sounded the same. We were also interviewed all day. One of my questions was,

"How many pennies does it cost to make a loaf of bread?" I said, "Three cents," and I was correct. Next, we had a luncheon with the judges in order for them to observe our table manners and etiquette. My father was from Missouri, and he was a stickler for manners. Due to my father's pride in proper manners, I was one of the few to actually know how to use a fork.

The last event was the evening banquet, and we were required to wear formal gowns. I was staying at a different hotel from the other competitors, because my family was also showing cattle at the State Dairy Show.

My mother was supposed to come to the hotel to help me get ready; however, she was busy helping with the cattle show. Now, I had a gown that had 39 buttons in the back, and I didn't have anyone to help me button them. I was going up and down the hallway looking for help until I found a lady who offered me her assistance. By this time, I was already running late. My brother picked me up, and we drove like crazy to get to the Crippled Children's Home for the banquet. My family and others were so anxious because I was late. I looked up at the head table and realized that the lady who had helped me with my dress was the wife of the President of the North Dakota Agricultural College. The President was going to do the honorary crowning due to the Governor being out of state. I was somewhat embarrassed to see her, because I had complained about my mom not being there to help me.

After the banquet, we were escorted to the Community Center in Jamestown for the coronation and Queen dance. Several of the contestants performed their talents at the ceremony.

So now we are ready for the coronation. I was seated in the back row, not being very serious, when my name was called. I cannot explain the feelings that I had at that time. It was indeed such an honor to be selected to represent the dairy industry and the State of North Dakota at 16 years of age.

After my coronation, my reign and a very busy schedule began. I attended numerous county fairs - - serving milk - - and also state meetings and banquets. I also went to Waterloo, Iowa, to attend the National Dairy Congress. I was introduced in the big arena, riding in the Budweiser wagon which was pulled by the Clydesdale horses. The Shetland ponies galloped right alongside.

From these wonderful honors, I have met many special people who have remained lifelong friends.

Shortly after I was crowned Dairy Queen, the name was changed to State Dairy Princess. Apparently, there were some trademark issues with the "Dairy Queen" stores that sell soft-serve ice cream.

Shirley Ann (Brown) Gummer and her husband raised beef cattle and small grains in North Dakota until 1999. She has five grandchildren and one great-grandchild. She has been active as a cattle judge, princess judge, and serves as the Chairman of the North Dakota State Milk Marketing board.

Hawkeye Dairy Farm in 1960 in Ruthven, Iowa.
Photo courtesy of Dolores Chapman-Tanner.

Iowa's First Dairy Princess

Dolores Chapman–Tanner

Iowa Dairy Princess of 1955

I grew up on a dairy farm in Northwest Iowa, near the little town of Ruthven. Our farm, Hawkeye Dairy Farm - - named for Iowa, the Hawkeye State - - sits on beautiful green rolling hills of corn, soybeans and alfalfa. We raised black and white registered Holstein cattle.

I was the oldest of five children. Mother and Dad were both 4-H club leaders, so we "kids" all had 4-H calves and heifers of our own to nurture (and love) and show at County, District, and State Fairs. Dairy was such a big part of our lives . . . and the slogan, "It's better with butter," was a favorite saying of our dad. Homemade ice cream was a frequent treat and is still my favorite dessert today! We still make it in a wooden tub freezer, but unlike the hand-crank freezer of yesteryear, ours is electric!

We got very attached to the calves, heifers, and cows that we worked with, groomed, and showed at fairs. They became like pets to us. I especially remember two beautiful heifers: "Starlet" and "Canary," both of which won quite a few blue ribbons and that I loved very much. Well . . . so did two cattle buyers (one from Canada, and one from California) who wanted to buy them to add to their cattle herds. I thought

I would die! When they came with their trucks to take them away, many tears were shed. My dad had a hard time convincing me that our heifers would be happy where they were going, but the dairy cattle and milk business, after all, was the way we made our living!

The "biggest event" in the history of our herd of cattle was when our 14-year-old prize cow, Constance Korndyke Veeman (nicknamed "Connie"), set a National Milk Production Record in 1953. Photographers came out to our farm to take pictures of her for newspapers and dairy magazines, and she was presented with a huge bouquet of red roses! After such an honor, she was given a special stall of her own, where she lived to the ripe old age of 18 years. She is buried out there on the farm, where my nephew David and his family now live and still raise and show registered Holsteins. They are the 4th generation to continue that farming tradition.

My dad died in 1993. Every year since then, my mother - - now 93 years old - - and I go with a third family member and present a silver tray to the Grand Champion Female cow, in my dad's memory, at the State Holstein Show.

In June of 1955, when I was 19 years old, I was crowned Iowa's First Dairy Princess. My title was "Golden Girl of Iowa." What a fun and exciting year it was! It was fun meeting people all over the country, as well as promoting something I loved so much! A $500 scholarship was also part of the honor, which helped with my college tuition at Drake

University in Des Moines, where I was majoring in Music & Education. Five hundred dollars was a "huge" amount toward college expenses 54 years ago! Needless to say, 1955 was a whirlwind of publicity for me, just as it had been for our famous "Connie cow" two years before!

I wouldn't trade my experiences of growing up on a dairy farm for anything in the world. The values of hard work, teamwork, love of the land and its natural beauty, love of and compassion for animals, as well as a sense of pride in caring for, showing and competing with animals are invaluable! (How beautiful they always looked when we led them into the show ring!)

Winning the Iowa Princess title was a very special time in my life. However, to paraphrase a well-known book title . . . "All I Need to Know, I Learned on a Dairy Farm!"

Dolores Chapman–Tanner has worked as a teacher and is currently the Christian Education Director at First United Methodist Church in Mason City, Iowa. She and her husband raised three children and now have three grandsons just five minutes away. She enjoys playing the piano, working with children (teaching and singing), gardening, and antiquing.

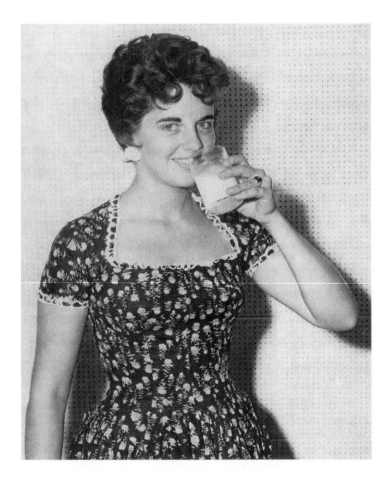

Dolores Chapman, 1955 Iowa Dairy Princess.
Photo courtesy of the Iowa Dairy Producers.

May Day Ruse

Karen Bright Carey

Iowa Dairy Princess of 1958

"The cows are out!" That phrase was not a statement, but a call to action. We heard those words from our parents many times throughout the years. And one memorable time was one year on May 1.

Our herd numbered around 50 purebred Brown Swiss, and each one was known not only by name but also by personality. They were part of the family, and each night Dad would go to the barn and tuck them in.

Our family worked together feeding, milking, showing, and pampering our prized herd. Dad worked hard and expected the same of each member of the family. He also loved to play and was a master of practical jokes, which set the tone for our lives. Sometimes he tricked a member of the family, and other times, family members would be in on the joke.

It was on the night of May 1st, during my 16th year, that I was waiting for my boyfriend to pick me up for a date. It was past dusk, so when he arrived the yard light was on, and he could see people running around "chasing cows." Of course, he went to help "get the cows in." He was not a slacker and wanted to help wherever he could.

What a shock he had when my mother grabbed him from out of the shadows and kissed him!

The cows weren't really loose. You see, May 1 is the holiday "May Day," and my parents' friends had brought a basket of food, set it at the front door and yelled "MAY BAS-KET," and then ran to hide. Our response was to run and catch them and invite them in to share the goodies. And my boyfriend was just caught in the middle of our fun.

Karen Bright Carey was crowned as the Iowa Dairy Princess in 1958. She moved to Denver after college, where she and her husband raised five children. She now enjoys her three grandchildren and will have five by this fall.

Karen Bright Carey, with a nephew sitting on a favorite cow in 1959. *Photo courtesy of Karen Bright Carey.*

Grandma's Miracle

Shelby Bohnenkamp

North Dakota Dairy Princess of 2008

The first thing I did when I got home from the parade that I had ridden in that day was jump out of my car and yell, "Hi, guys!" to the herd of cattle across the road from our house. Some people might think it's a little weird to say "hello" to a pen full of cattle, but I had always done that ever since I was a little girl. No one could convince me that our cattle wouldn't want to be treated kindly, just like any person would want. After all, I had our cattle to thank for the crown that was now sitting proudly on my head. I had been fortunate enough to win the 2008 North Dakota Dairy Princess competition just a month earlier at the North Dakota State Fair.

I ran up the steps to our door after I had greeted the cattle, a kindness that I'm sure they would have returned if they could have! Some families probably always use their front door. However, most farm families usually use a different door that leads to a porch or mudroom when they have their barn clothes on. Although I was wearing my crown, sash, and a sundress, I still used our mudroom door. What can I say? Old habits die hard!

Anyway, I went to my room right away to change. In strong contrast to the new, flowing sundress that I had worn for the parade earlier that afternoon, I pulled on a pair of old, faded jeans and an ancient t-shirt that I just couldn't bring myself to part with. It felt pretty good to slip my feet into my cowboy boots after wearing strappy, high-heeled sandals since early that morning. The last part of my "princess" outfit that I took off was my favorite piece: my crown. It means so much to me. I feel like whenever I wear it I have this amazing ability to accomplish good things and have a positive impact on the people around me. So I always keep my crown on as long as possible. At last, I carefully removed it from my hair and set it down on top of my nightstand, right beside my bed. Then I pulled on my old Land O' Lakes cap and pulled my long hair into a ponytail through the back of the cap.

I was in a hurry today because one of my favorite old milk cows was about to calve. That morning, before the parade, my parents had told me that this cow had looked sick during the morning chores. She had been off by herself and acting very uncomfortable. It's normal for cows that are about to calve to sometimes act like this, but my dad hadn't thought that this cow was that close to calving.

This particular cow had a very special meaning to my family. She was born many years ago on the morning of my grandma's funeral. This might sound somewhat disturbing to a lot of people, but dairy cattle had always been a huge part of my family's way of life. My grandparents on my dad's side went to a sale barn and bought about 20 Holstein heifer calves when my dad was just a little kid. My dad's family worked to raise those heifers and keep them healthy. Over time, those original 20 calves added their own offspring to our herd, and my dad and grandpa also bought more dairy cattle to increase our herd size.

So it was kind of fitting that a little Holstein heifer calf was born on the morning of my grandma's funeral. It was one of the cutest little calves I had ever seen. She was predominantly white with a few small, black spots on her face and sides. However, on the morning of my grandma's funeral, the last thing that most of us had wanted was a newborn calf. Everyone was hurrying to get chores done and make it to the morning service. Not to mention, it had been an emotionally trying day, for obvious reasons.

This little calf, which had chosen a really inconvenient time to come into the world, would become a very important part of our farm and our lives. We named her "Grandma" as a tribute to my grandma. My sister and I had been little kids at the time she was born. So, of course, we took it upon ourselves to raise this calf. We halter broke her and would take her out for walks across the yard.

Grandma did get to lead pretty well, which was lucky since my sister decided to take her to the county fair that fall. At the fair, they had a contest called "Critters in Costumes," in which the animal and the handler would dress up in matching costumes. What else could we dress Grandma up as but a grandmother? We made a sort of dress out of a flowered sheet and altered a floppy straw hat to tie onto her head. To really complete the look, my sister dressed up as a grandpa.

So my family has a lot of really fond memories with our cow named "Grandma." That's why we were all a little bit worried when she started acting like she might be sick.

As I walked out into the pasture behind our milk barn, I could see Grandma off lying by herself. She was flat out on her side and obviously very miserable. I ran over to her side and knelt down by her head.

I could see her big, scared eye turn and look right at me. It was like she was asking me to help her. Despite myself, I couldn't help but begin to cry. I immediately dug my cell phone out of my jeans pocket and called my dad. He had gone out to the field after he and my mom returned from the parade.

I told him that "Grandma" was down on her side and looked really bad. He said that he'd call the veterinarian and would come in from the field as soon as he could. Unfortunately, the field that he was in is quite a distance from our house.

I knew that it would take a little while before either my dad or the veterinarian would get there. So I sat cross-legged by Grandma's head and petted the side of her face. Even if I couldn't really help her right away, maybe I'd at least be able to calm her down.

After sitting there for a little while, I thought I heard a noise. The sound was muffled, and I couldn't really tell what it was. I figured it must be a bird or something.

Then, "Grandma" started to act like she was trying to moo, but no noise would come out. I could tell that she was getting weaker by the minute. She could hardly even lift her head off the grass anymore. I just sat there by her, trying not to cry too hard, and kept stroking her head. I just wanted to make sure that she knew I was there for her.

Suddenly, Grandma made a swinging motion with her legs in one last attempt to get up. I even had to back up in order to avoid getting hit by her big swinging head. For a minute, I thought that she might be able to get her feet underneath her and stand up. But she just fell back down to the ground. I ran back over to her. Her eyes were looking right at me, and then they closed for the last time.

As much as I didn't want it to be true, I knew that "Grandma" was gone. I leaned my head on her neck and started to sob. Then I heard the same noise that I had heard earlier. Except this time it was a little bit louder and sounded like it was coming from the grass about 50 feet away.

I looked in the direction of the noise and stood up and began to search for its source. As I got closer, I began to recognize what it sounded like. It had to be a newborn baby calf! I had heard that sound enough times that I could recognize it anywhere.

I began to jog toward the source of the noise and couldn't believe my eyes. There, sunk deep into the tall grass, was a little, white Holstein calf. She was trying to stand up for the first time.

I was so in shock that all I could do for a little while was stare at this little calf. Obviously, "Grandma" had given us one last gift before she'd gone. I went over to the calf and helped lift her up so that she would be able to stand. I might not have been able to help Grandma, but I could sure try to help her calf.

This little calf turned its head and stared at me with the curiosity that only a new baby that has not yet seen any of the world has. I reached down and petted her on the head. She was so little and looked just liked her mother.

By the time my dad and the veterinarian got there, the little calf was following me all over the pasture. I told them about Grandma and how I'd found the calf. They were both upset about Grandma but glad that the calf seemed to be perfectly healthy.

The little, white calf would become almost as much of a baby as "Grandma" had been. And what else could we name her but "Miracle"? This just goes to show that sometimes when something really bad happens, it means that something else good is about to happen. The ending of one story is always the beginning of another…

Shelby Bohnenkamp is a student at NDSU (North Dakota State University), majoring in political science. Her career plans include law school. When not studying, she enjoys horseback riding, reading, spending time with friends and family, scrapbooking, and helping on her family's dairy and beef cattle farm.

Shelby Bohnenkamp, North Dakota Dairy Princess of 2008.
Photo courtesy of Shelby Bohnenkamp.

2007 Princess Kay of the Milky Way
Ann Miron

When I reflect on the past year, I can't help but think to myself, "Why me?" Why was I given this wonderful opportunity? Why was I chosen to serve as Princess Kay of the Milky Way? Well, for whatever reason, here I am, flipping through four scrapbooks filled with the unforgettable memories of one amazing year. Each page of my scrapbooks represents an event in which I promoted the industry that I love. But the pages that fill these books are more than that. Each page is filled with faces - - the faces of people I met throughout this unforgettable year.

On one page is a newspaper clipping of the little smiling freckle-faced girl who meets a real princess for the first time. And on another is the teenage boy beaming with pride as he shows off his prize heifer at the county fair. In another book, there is a smiling woman, bubbling with excitement as she learns more about the dairy industry, across from the hard-working dairy farmer who opened up his farm to the community. And in yet another scrapbook is the photo of an elderly man who genuinely got to know me and shared his wisdom that had only ripened with time.

Over my Princess Kay year, I have had the privilege of meeting many dairy farmers. And although their ages and sizes of their farms differ, and they come from a variety of places, each dairy farm family shares a love for and dedication to their way of life. And this love shows through in everything that they do. You can see that love shining through when you look at their healthy cows and as they work and care for the land they call home. And you can see it in the wholesome product they produce. Dairy farmers are extraordinary.

As the 54th Princess Kay of the Milky Way I had the opportunity to share the dairy industry's good news everywhere I went. One of my favorite activities as Princess Kay was classroom visits. I really enjoyed all the questions that the students just had to ask. On one visit I was caught a bit off guard by a little girl's question. She asked me, "Are you a real princess? Do you live in a castle?" I explained to her that I was a real princess but I did not live in a castle. But, the more I thought about it, the more I began to see the similarities between a dairy farm and a beautiful castle. No, I don't live in the highest room in the tallest tower, but I have climbed the ladder to the top of the silo. And I don't go around kissing frogs to see if they're princes, but I have received a big slobbery wet one from my favorite cow. And I don't sleep on the finest linens or eat gourmet meals, but we do work hard to provide "luxuries" to our cows. This little girl not only reminded me how special it is to grow up on a dairy farm, she made me aware of the impact and impression that I could make as a dairy princess. She helped me to remember the day in which I realized I wanted to be a dairy princess.

It was a hot and humid day in August - - the kind where the air sticks to your skin. It was my first trip to the Minnesota State Fair, and there was so much I wanted to see and do. I was 10 years old and was taking in all of the sights and sounds around me. But unfortunately, I was stuck; I was glued to my dad's sweaty hand and standing on "Machinery Hill." My dad and brothers became entranced for hours by horse-power this and hydraulic that. I tried to be patient, but I was growing restless. I could feel my body squirming with excitement and so could my dad.

We finally started to move through the fairground. My eyes widened as I saw roller coasters, millions of people, and cows?! Yes, cows, as we were headed straight for the cattle barns. My dad saw some friends in one of the barns, and I knew we were going to be there for a while. So I began to examine the cattle, comparing them all with my favorite cows at home. That one did not have an udder like Pearl's and this one's feet and legs were nowhere near as well formed.

Before I knew it, I could feel my dad's damp hand grasp mine and we continued on our way. As we walked, my dad looked down at me, smiled, and said, "How would you like an ice cold malt?" I jumped with joy and we scurried to the Dairy Building. We worked our way through the crowd, and as we arrived in the back of the building the crowd parted. I looked up and was mesmerized by the beautiful dairy princess whose likeness was being carved in butter. I steadily walked straight for the butter booth like a dart to a bull's-eye. For the next half hour, my nose was pressed against the butter booth glass, only to be removed by that familiar guiding hand. I knew from that moment, I wanted to be a dairy princess and share my love for my animal friends back at home.

Ann Miron was the 2007 Princess Kay of the Milky Way in Minnesota. She is a junior at the University of Minnesota, majoring in Agricultural Education. She enjoys arts and crafts, and her favorite job on the farm is raking hay.

Anne Miron, 2007-2008 Princess Kay of the Milky Way with her butterhead. Photo © Patrick O'Leary, used with permission from the University of Minnesota.

The "Dear Dairy" in my Life

Amanda Messick

2008 Virginia Dairy Princess

June is "Dairy Month," and there are a lot of dairy-themed events going on all over the state of Virginia.

One very memorable event in my princess year was "Dairy Day" in Richmond, Virginia. This event took place inside a shopping mall, and there was a lot going on. They have a "Got Milk?" and "3-A-Day" tent where kids and adults can read about the benefits of including milk, cheese, and yogurt in their diets. (You can have your picture taken with a milk moustache.)

The cow-milking contest at "Dairy Day" is a big hit! A farm provides live cows in the middle of the shopping mall, to be milked by someone the farmer chooses. There were two "milking teams," and the team with the most milk in the bucket at the end of the allotted time would be the winner. Other than myself, nobody on my team knew how to milk a cow, so I first had to quickly show them all how to milk a cow by hand. The other team had the advantage, because a couple of them already knew how to milk. Unfortunately, my team lost, but it was really funny seeing grown men try to milk a Holstein cow, with milk flying in every direction! Even though we lost the contest, my teammates all had a great time and learned something new.

My favorite cattle breed has always been the Holstein. You know how scientists say "nobody has the same fingerprint?" Well, that is the same with the Holstein cow, and their black and white patches...no Holstein cows have the same exact pattern! Their patterns are all unique, just like a human's fingerprint; it's their own identity.

Ever since I was a little girl, living on a dairy farm was my life. It was second nature for me to go and help my dad feed the little baby Holstein calves every day. I have to say growing up on a dairy farm has molded me into the person I am today; I can't even think what my life would be like without the farm.

During the summer, I would be on a tractor for hours, working in the fields, helping my family as much as possible. I learned to drive a tractor at the age of 10, and who can say they have known how to drive stick shift since they were 10? Sometimes I would even go and help milk the cows, but we had enough hired help that it eventually became unnecessary.

My brother, sister, and I are the 4th generation on the dairy farm, and we're very proud of it. I would have to say the best part about living on a dairy farm is the newborn calves -- walking into the barn and hearing all of the little ones start mooing because they know it's time to be fed. There are a few babies that don't get the idea to drink out of a bucket, so you have to bottle-feed them, and then try the bucket again.

Being away at college and far away from home has really impacted me. I miss going to the farm and helping my family. I now know what my life would have been like without the farm: empty. It's my passion, my family history; it's my life.

Amanda Messick was the 2008 Virginia Dairy Princess, after serving as Virginia Dairy Duchess in 2007. She is a freshman at Johnson & Wales University. She loves to sing, play volleyball, scrapbook, and ride her dirt bike around the family property.

Amanda Messick, 2008 Virginia Dairy Princess.
Photo courtesy of Amanda Messick.

Milking Cows with the I-Cubs

Jennifer Zumbach

Iowa Dairy Princess Alternate, 1998 - 1999

In the summer of 1999, while serving as the Iowa Dairy Princess Alternate, I had the exciting opportunity to throw out the first pitch at an I-Cubs baseball game in Des Moines, Iowa. While this event doesn't normally include cows, they made an exception for my appearance.

The Iowa State University Dairy Science Club runs a booth called "I Milked a Cow," which is usually held at the Iowa State Fair, where State Fair goers can try their hand at hand milking a cow!

At the I-Cubs game, in conjunction with the Midwest Dairy Association, they brought four dairy cows from the University to the ball game for a little cow-milking contest that day, pitting me against three I-Cub baseball players: a catcher and two pitchers. I must admit that I thought I could easily win the contest!

As I eyed the four cows, I noticed that a couple of them looked like they would soon be going dry, and would not have as much milk as the other two. I edged my way over to my preferred cow: the Jersey, representing my favorite breed, and also looking to have the fullest udder of the four cows.

As I moved in toward the Jersey, the contest "officials" pointed to the cow that I was to have on my "team" - - a very "stale looking" Ayrshire!!! I took my place at a milking stool next to my designated cow. I had my work cut out for me! We would be given exactly one minute to squeeze as much milk as we could into a container for volume comparison. I'm not sure if the surrounding fans were prepared for the entertainment they were in for!

An official yelled, "Start!" and with the fans loudly cheering us on, I tried my hardest to incorporate the system I learned over the years of milking "fresh" cows by hand. I knew that my classmates and instructors would not let me live down a loss to three baseball players who'd probably never milked a cow in their lives!

The Ayrshire on my "team" must have been milked right before they brought the cows in!! She wasn't interested in helping a dairy princess win the competition! One grueling minute later, the results were being tallied as the milk was dumped into a measuring flask. Although I tried my best, I came in a close second to the catcher. The two pitchers didn't fare as well!

Jennifer Zumbach and her husband, Dave, live in Hopkinton, Iowa. They continue to farm with both of their families on their farms: Jennifer helps in milking 150 Jerseys and Dave works to feed out 900 Holstein steers per year. Jennifer is the Secretary/Treasurer of the Iowa Jersey Cattle Club. She also coaches for county 4-H Dairy Quiz Bowl teams and sings at weddings.

Living my Childhood Dream

Merideth (Weiderspahn) Riddle

1996-1997 Crawford County Dairy Princess

1996-1997 Pennsylvania 1st Alternate Dairy Princess

Favorite Cow: Wright-Way Bonanza Havilah, aka Havilah

As a young girl, I remember the first time I saw a dairy princess riding on a shiny, silver milk truck in a parade. The sight of the beautifully adorned princess perched high upon her cylindrical throne is forever etched in my mind. The metallic gleam of the polished stainless steel milk tank was rivaled only by the dairy princess's tiara as it glittered in the sun. Every fiber of my being wanted to be that girl!

After several years of longingly watching that first dairy princess and her successors riding happily aloft the milk truck in parades, a wonderful thing happened… my parents bought a dairy farm. Not only did this monumental event qualify me to someday compete for the title of dairy princess, it also afforded this little girl the opportunity to practice her princess wave while perched atop a tall moving vehicle.

Each summer I would eagerly look forward to helping my dad bale hay. This was not because I loved working the earth, nor was it because I liked to work side by side with my father as his little helper. No, the reason I eagerly awaited haying season was because of what happened once the wagon was piled high with those scratchy green bales. I would climb to the uppermost bale of hay and perch myself upon my makeshift milk truck. Once safely on top of the mountain of hay, my dad would begin the slow voyage back to the hay mow to unload the bounty.

As we journeyed back to the barn, I would imagine that the path through the field was actually a busy street along a parade route. I would practice my princess grin and grace-fully wave to my mom, younger brother, grandparents, and the dog that walked with us along the "parade route."

One day all of my daydreaming and waving practice finally paid off. In the summer after I turned 16, I ran for my county's dairy princess title. Once I had finally earned my crown, I couldn't wait to realize my childhood fantasy of rid-ing upon a *real* milk truck. As my first parade drew near, I was educated by the retiring dairy princess on the secret art of riding a milk truck. Little had I known how very far off my youthful imaginings had been!

The first thing I was given was an old, stained, rubber bath mat with suction cups on the bottom. It had been used by several of my predecessors to secure a better grip on the rounded top of the milk tank. I was then instructed that a for-mal dress with a full skirt that would fan out was a must. What I was to wear under that dress was perhaps the most important of all. Shorts worn under the dress were absolutely necessary in order to keep a princess's decency during the ascent to the top of the truck. I was also instructed that bare legs, and not panty hose, were the proper accompaniment to a formal dress when riding on a stainless steel milk tank. While bare legs did feel the heat of the sunbathed metal, they provided for an excellent grip on the metal surface. (In fact, I later hypothesized that human perspiration undergoes a chemical reaction when introduced to polished stainless steel to create a bonding agent.)

After more than a decade of waiting and dreaming, my first parade day finally arrived. I took painstaking measures to ensure that I was properly dressed for my maiden voyage atop the milk truck. It was a beautiful, sunny, July day with a gentle breeze. I arrived at the parade lineup to be greeted by a cherry red 16-wheeler hauling the most magnificent, glistening, silver milk tank I had ever laid eyes on! It was a thing of resplendent beauty, and it was calling my name.

With great anticipation and trembling fingers, I began my climb up the ladder to the crest of the milk truck. Once perched high upon my metallic throne, I took a deep breath and sucked in the sweet air of achievement. After several minutes, the floats ahead of us started inching their way along the parade route. This was my moment to shine!

But without warning, the milk truck jerked forward with the grace of a circus elephant balancing on a ball. I gripped the top of the ladder with white knuckles in order to keep from reeling backward. I was again thankful for the shorts I was wearing under my formal. (Having since learned to drive a "standard," I have forgiven the driver of that semi truck. I realize now that smooth starts and stops are too much to ask of a semi hauling a full load.)

I decided then and there to wrap my bare legs around the tops of the ladders to balance myself better. This action worked to stabilize myself for the first several blocks of starts and stops along the parade route. But just as I was beginning to feel comfortable enough to enjoy my long-awaited moment, something I had not expected happened.

The parade route turned from a side street in town onto one of the main roads at a key intersection. I was focused on straddling the tank and waving to my adoring parade goers. Suddenly, the crowd on the sidewalk began yelling and pointing. Confused, I turned in the direction they were yelling.

At that moment, my life flashed before my eyes in the form of a three-foot-tall, yellow traffic light. I gasped and lunged to the side, again thankful for the shorts I was wearing under my dress. The adrenaline coursing through my body left me jittery and shaken for the remainder of the parade. Apparently, while making the left-hand turn, the driver of the truck miscalculated the position of the traffic light in relation to where I was precariously perched atop the milk tank!

When the milk truck finally pulled to a halt in the parking lot at the conclusion of the parade, I scrambled to get down. I descended the ladder with fingers trembling yet again. Once I had both feet firmly planted on solid ground, I turned to my mom. Unsure of whether to laugh or cry, I chose the first option. With a tremor in my voice, I announced my decision to limit my parade rides to convertibles and hay wagons in open fields.

I lived my childhood dream that warm afternoon and have no regrets of doing so. Because of my experience as a dairy princess, I learned an important life lesson that July in 1996: *set lofty goals, but watch out for traffic lights!*

Merideth (Weiderspahn) Riddle grew up in rural northwestern Pennsylvania. She is now teaching fifth grade in a rural community about 45 minutes away from her parents' dairy farm. Her husband is a pastor at a growing church in the area. Their two young daughters enjoy spending time at Nana and Papa's farm, playing in the barn and helping tend to the many farm animals.

Merideth Weiderspan, 1996-1997
Crawford County Dairy Princess;
1996-1997 Pennsylvania 1st Alternate Dairy Princess.
Photo courtesy of Merideth (Weiderspahn) Riddle.

Cattle Sillies

"When a cow laughs, does milk come out her nose?"

~ Author Unknown

The Heifer That Rolled Me

Hank Pool

One spring I purchased a young Hereford heifer from a rancher, right out of a range herd. My plan was to fatten her up for beef. Well, she was pretty wild, but I somehow managed to get her loaded into the back of my pickup.

When we got her home, I wrestled a halter onto her before opening the tailgate. A couple of neighbor men happened by and were watching me fasten the halter when the heifer jumped out and the "rodeo" started.

The heifer was bucking and jumping while I was trying to get her through a wire gate and into the pasture. We were both going around in circles, and then the two of us got tangled up with the wire gate. We both went slamming down and rolled around on the ground before the heifer suddenly jerked me back up. One fellow yelled, "Hang on!" and the other yelled, "Let go!"   I didn't have much choice either way, as things were happening so fast.

When she finally paused for her second wind, we managed to get ourselves untangled from each other and the gate, and I managed to get her into the pasture. The two neighbor men were laughing so hard that they were absolutely no help.

Both of my shoulders were dislocated and I had bruises up and down both arms. And in the end, the worst of it was that when we did butcher this heifer, the meat was tough and tasted just terrible. I guess she got the last laugh!

Henry "Hank" Pool grew up on a dairy farm near Maple Plain, Minnesota. He served in the Maritime Service in the mid-'40s and as an Army medic during the Korean War. Following his military service, he raised quarter horses on an 80-acre ranch and was an electrician in Livingston, Montana, where he married and raised two sons. He currently resides in northeastern Washington.

How to Feed the Chickadees in Winter

Marion Greveling

1. Fill a pail with cracked grains. (I used oats, barley, and wheat, but you can use any combination that you have.) I filled up a whole pail so I could feed the cattle as well. Cattle are not mandatory to feed chickadees, but without the cattle I wouldn't have fed the chickadees. You'll find out....

2. Fill up another pail with whole grains. (I used oats, barley, and wheat again, but feel free to substitute your grain of choice.) *Note:* This has nothing to do with chickadees, but you might as well feed the sheep and "Roger the goat" on your way past them.

3. Start walking down the hill to where the cattle, sheep, and "Roger the goat" live.

4. Just when you get close to the cattle, slip on the ice, shriek, and fall down with a plop!

5. Lie there for awhile to catch your breath and see if your hip is okay. By now the cattle are mooing. You might think this means in "cowspeak," "Are you okay? That was a nasty fall." What it really means is, "Get your butt off the ice and get over here with our grain." Those big, brown, bovine eyes look soft and caring, but they are really just concerned about their food.

6. Get up, rub your butt, and try to pick as much grain off the snow as you can. It's only the cracked grain that spills; the pail with the whole grain in it never spills. (You can try it for yourself, but so far I never spill the whole grain, and I have fed the chickadees this way at least four times this winter.)

7. Tell the cows to stop mooing at you. Climb over the electric fence and clean the snow out of the trough. Be careful while you do this. The cattle are curious and like to get their heads in where yours is. They have big heads - - big, hard heads. Without any exaggeration, their heads are even bigger and harder than yours or mine. Tell the cows they could have cleaned the trough out themselves and that would speed up the process. Clean the first trough again, because "Conway" has stepped in it and filled it back up with snow. Put the cracked grain in the trough for the cattle and step away before they step on your toes. (Remember the bull in the china shop? There is a reason we don't have a cow named "Grace." We do have a goat named "Grace"- - but I digress.)

8. Climb over the electric fence by the sheep and "Roger the goat." Clean the snow out of their trough. Watch "Roger" all of the time. (He has horns and he knows how to use them.) He has never hit a human being, but he hits the sheep, which will then bounce off you. It's like playing pool for Roger, except he doesn't use a pool cue! He just bunts a sheep, the sheep bounces into the farmer, and the farmer goes in the corner trough. Something like

that anyways, I don't really know how to play pool. I just know Roger. Maybe Roger thinks it's "snooker." I don't even know the difference.

9. Pour the whole grains in for the sheep and "Roger the goat." They will crowd all around you, and now you can hardly get away. At least they are warm and wooly pressed up tight to your legs. You can't fall down now; they are holding you up. They are also stepping on your toes, but 150 pounds of sheep on your toes is okay. Way better than 1600 pounds of bovine on your toes (see #7).

10. Climb back over the electric fence. Use the inside of your thigh to test the fence. Yup, it's working just fine. You can shriek again during the "fence test." I usually do, but that's just me.

11. Look over to where you first fell on the ice. See the chickadees happily eating the rest of the spilled grain out of the snow. They are very efficient grain cleaner-uppers. Now you can go in for your own breakfast, since everybody, even the chickadees, has been fed.

Marion Greveling lives in Ontario, Canada, on a dairy sheep farm with her husband, four children, and ruminant animals, both large and small. She enjoys gardening, making sheep's milk cheese, and attending the local farmer's market.

Close Encounters: Alvin & Margie

Kermit H. Dietrich

I worked for Alvin and Ella Sook of rural Buffalo, Minnesota, during summers while I was in high school. A big part of my job was to help with the milking.

Alvin was an Irishman with a volatile temper that quickly cooled. He also had a wonderful sense of humor that was always directed at himself, and never at others.

We were milking the cows with the old Surge bucket milking machines. Alvin was crouched down, attaching a machine, when old Margie, the cow behind him, raised her left leg and her foot came down between his belt and his backside.

The next minute was a flurry of activity with Margie bucking wildly, with Alvin buckled to her leg with his leather belt. After my initial shock, I helped get them separated and we determined that neither of them was injured by the experience.

As I reviewed the scene in my mind, I could not contain my laughter. Then Alvin turned beet red from the top of his bald head, and I feared for my life, but couldn't stop laughing. Then Alvin started laughing too, until both of us were crying.

Alvin would recall this story many times in later years when we got together. I will always remember his infectious laughter that seemed to start in his shoes and shake his whole body.

******

At Alvin and Ella's dispersal auction, Alvin pointed out the granddaughter of old Margie. She was named Margie, too.

Kermit H. Dietrich is a retired dairy farmer and U.S. Navy submarine veteran living in Waconia, Minnesota. He has taught English as a Second Language and currently volunteers at the Carver County Historical Museum. He is now an artist and enjoys painting.

"Natasha" © Kermit H. Dietrich

Bull at Play

Becky Iciek

We still run a bull for breeding our heifers. One time we had this big black one, getting a bit "on in years." We usually get rid of them before they turn two years old. That's about the time they discover they are a bull, with everything that means.

One day we were cleaning out the cattle shelter with a loader tractor. My husband had set the round bale feeder on edge to make it easier to move as needed. (If you have never seen one of these, it's a gigantic metal ring - - usually red, about 10 feet in diameter, into which a giant round hay bale is dropped.)

The bull discovered that when he bumped it, it would roll. Well, he decided this was great fun. He bumped it one way and then followed it around and bumped it back the other direction. This guy was playing with the round baler just like a kid with a toy! It was hilarious.

But what really got us laughing was when it finally fell over on the flat side. He jumped back because of the sound and then pushed it again. Nothing happened. So he went around to the other side and tried pushing it again. Of course it didn't roll this time either. Then he looked at the round baler for a few seconds and turned back his head to look at us like, "Hey, what happened? Where'd my fun go?" My husband and I just rolled.

Becky Iciek was born in Denver, Colorado, in 1952. She married Mark Iciek in 1974 and began dairy farming in 1990 with her husband and six children. They started with 30 cows and eight calves and now milk 200 cows and raise all heifers. They have four dogs, many cats, 25 geese, and love the country life.

Cow Poetry

Never kick a cow chip on a hot day.

~Proverb

THE COW

The cow is of the bovine ilk;
One end is moo, the other, milk.

Ogden Nash (1902-1971)

The New Cow

The new cow came through the gate,
And her calf came after, a little late.
No longer willing to be led,
The calf went on ahead,
While she stood to look around
Over the hills and lower ground
Stood shyly, defiantly there,
Smelling flower-fragrant air,
And gazed toward the old cows
Grouped on the way before.
Knowing not how she might stay
Among them, stranger still,
She hesitated yet, now they had turned
At the foot of the hill
And seemed to wait for her at the gate,
To wait for her who was strange and thin,
Til she came on,
And they opened their ranks
To take her in.

August Derleth
(1909-1971)

You see an old barn

I retrieve memories
A little red tractor
80 acres of farmland
A hardworking man in a Sears denim jacket

Herds of cows
"Don't feed them too much clover
It's not good for them," he'd say.
Later, there were sheep
Bottle-fed lambs in the kitchen

Lunch time;
Go in for homemade noodles
My grandma in a flower print dress,
Apron tied neatly across

A spotless farm house
Two levels, extra bedrooms upstairs
Don't dangle pencils through the grate
You'll get in trouble

Look out the 2nd floor window
There's the big tree
With the swing
Toby, the cat, stalked mice
And kept the farm free of pests
He also liked to bat a walnut
Around the kitchen, in play

It's all gone now
Time goes on
People die
Things change

But memories last forever.

Linda Schumacher blschue@verizon.net   *First printed at*
http://prairiehome.publicradio.org/

The Cow

The friendly cow all red and white,
    I love with all my heart:
She gives me cream with all her might,
    To eat with apple-tart.

She wanders lowing here and there,
    And yet she cannot stray,
All in the pleasant open air,
    The pleasant light of day;

And blown by all the winds that pass
    And wet with all the showers,
She walks among the meadow grass
    And eats the meadow flowers.

Robert Louis Stevenson
(1850–1894)

First printed in 1885 under the title *Penny Whistles*, later
entitled *A Child's Garden of Verses.*

Teaching a Calf to Drink

The hardest thing on a farm, I think
Is trying to teach a calf to drink.

You pull and haul, get his head in a pail;
He'll stand there and twist and wiggle his tail;
And the very first thing, *kerplunk* goes his nose,
and most of the milk goes over your clothes!

Hang onto your patience, your teeth you must grit;
If you can't hold your temper, you might as well quit,
For mother nature, whose methods don't fail,
Never meant for a calf to drink from a pail.

Back him into a corner, straddle his neck;
He won't damage you much, you're already a wreck.
Just give him a finger, and maybe, with luck
That little old rascal will start in to suck.

Pick up your bucket and push his head down,
Then away you go again, around and around;
Just do this a week with your back in a kink,
And maybe by then you'll teach him to drink.

Anonymous

Provided by the Iowa Jersey Cattle Club

Purple Cow poem by Frank Gelett Burgess. Image from
San Francisco's *The Lark* volume 1, number 1
(May 1, 1895).

The 4-H Show

I had a Jersey Heifer, I thought her very fine
I tied her in the loafing shed, for she was really mine
I had her as my project, in our local 4-H club
I polished up her horns and gave a daily rub
Her hide did shine, her horns looked nice
I trimmed her hooves, not once but twice
The show came along with our county fair
Each boy led out, the judge to pass
Each one secretly hoping, that he'd top the class
We led in a circle, with the judge standing by
Analyzing the heifers, 'till one caught his eye
He beckoned one forth, and then two and then three
I thought surely then, he'd beckon to me
But alas, 'twas not so, another did call
I felt so bad, I wanted to bawl
But as a 4-H boy, I must be a sport
Stick out the battle, and stay at the fort
The judge kept looking and pulling them in
My heart was so heavy, but I tried hard to grin
There was one left to place, and that one was me
I would be placed last, 'twas easy to see
He looked at my heifer, then gave me a smile
And publicly announced that she had much style
He'd saved this heifer, he thought her so fine
That he wanted her to stand at the head of the line
I wanted to weep; I was so full of joy
I want you to know, I was the happiest boy

Ivan N. Gates (1908 – 1995)

Cow Haikus

Who can I moo to
when my four stomachs rumble?
hey you, in blue jeans!

Behold the Holsteins
black on white, or red on white
both ways are spotted.

In ancient Europe
belted bovine breeds arose
with their one white stripe.

C. R. Lindemer

Cattle Escapes

"Never take the Bull bi the horns Yung Man, but take him bi the tale. Then yu kan let go when yu want to."

Josh Billings (1818 - 1885)
American humorist and lecturer,
author of *Old Farmer's Allminax*

Ole "Red"

Clint Kepferle

The summer of 1983 brought about desert-dreary boredom on the ranch we lived on in Arizona. One particular day my younger brother and I decided we were going to catch and ride the skittish new steer we called "Red," a two-year-old, lanky-built Texas Longhorn.

This was something that never would have been allowed by our parents. We raised cattle to sell at auction. (Cattle don't gain weight when they get a lot of exercise.)

Our folks were away at work. And we had all of our chores done and had the rest of the day to ourselves.

After cornering "Red," and with my newfound roping talent, I managed to get the rope cinched around his long horns. In an instant, "Red" shot past me, heading out to the two open acres next to our house.

I was still holding the rope. In that split second, two thoughts flashed in my mind: "This is gonna hurt," and "We're gonna be in trouble for this!"

The thing I didn't think about was letting go of the rope. That rope burned its way through my hands until it reached the knot at the end, and I held on. Immediately, I was on my belly being dragged across the sandy, rocky, scrub brush terrain that comprised our property. As I was being dragged past my younger brother, he jumped on my back in an effort to help. It didn't.

I would say that steer dragged us for about 200 feet before it dawned on me to let go of the rope. When I got up and looked myself over, I was scraped up from my face to my feet, my hands were a bloody mess, and my clothes were torn to shreds. We no longer felt the need to ride that steer, but started thinking about getting that rope off him, making up a story, and calling it a day before our folks got home, which was easier said than done.

My brother and I commenced with chasing that steer around the property for the next five hours until finally, "Red" gave out and collapsed. The closest we could get to him was the end of the rope. Any closer and he'd get up and move away. We were all exhausted, so I grabbed the end of the rope and flipped it until it came loose from the steer's horns. And as quick as we could, we got the rope put away and went to throw away our shredded clothes and get cleaned up.

I was in the barn when my mother showed up asking, "What happened to 'Red?'" Of course we told her we didn't know. I could tell that she knew, by the condition I was in, but she didn't tell our dad. I guess she figured I'd been punished enough.

That steer lay out in the pasture all night, but by morning he was back on his feet, appearing none the worse for wear, which is more than I could say for myself. (Had he not survived, I might not be here to tell this story.)

Nothing was ever again said about "the incident"; however, my brother and I had a lot more chores to do after that. The two of us still laugh about it sometimes, but that was one daredevil stunt we never attempted again!

Clint Kepferle is 37, married to Christina, and has six children: five girls and a boy. He lives in the Kansas City (cow town) area. He is employed as a truck driver and owns a small electroplating business. Making peoples' personal items beautiful is his passion. He also holds a degree in Private Investigation.

Shoot to Kill

J. Daniel Rohrer

One Monday in February, about seven years ago, my dad was out working around the farm. His truck backfired a couple of times, and the dozen calves in our lean-to took off with a start, crashing through the electric fence and running off with their tails up in the air. Dad got them all back in, fixed a break in the fence, and called it a day.

On Tuesday, at morning chore time, no calves were to be found. It seemed that they had broken the fence in a couple of places, and Dad had patched up only one of the spots. We looked around and followed their tracks in the snow. They appeared to have circled the farm and paused in several spots where the boundary fence turned them back. (The fence wasn't electrified, but they knew enough to have respect for it!) Unfortunately, at some point they came to a spot where the snow had taken the fence down and they had sauntered on over it.

We tracked them halfway across a neighbor's field, where we saw them running, but from there we lost them. Later on that day, Dad called me at work to let me know what was up. I called a couple of my co-workers and told them to keep their eyes open for my calves.

At about 3:30 that afternoon, one of my buddies called to tell me he had spotted my calves about six miles from my home! I didn't believe him until he described the biggest black one - - 1100 pounds and close to market-ready - - and the smallest one of the bunch, a sickly calf.

I raced out there and began to try and herd them back toward home. Night was falling and I had moved them about a mile into a pretty deep, brushy marsh area where I thought they'd be safe.

I got a call from a guy at about 10:00 p.m. He said that my cattle had just come thundering by his place, about three miles west of where I had left them. I felt sick.

Dawn on Wednesday came clear and cold. It never got up above 10 degrees Fahrenheit. We headed toward where we'd last heard about the loose herd. After circling the edge of our city of 15,000 a couple of times, we found the calves resting under a willow tree, right up against a guy's backyard! I got ahold of as many of the guys from work and neighbors as I could find. I went home and loaded up a couple of bags of feed and all of the gates I had that weren't nailed down.

Before I got back, one of the guys called me in a panic to tell me that the herd had started running the "wrong way" on the state highway, headed right into town. The guys managed to head them off as they ran back through the St. Charles Furniture parking lot. They got the calves back across the highway and into some wasteland near the edge of town.

At that point the county sheriff showed up. All we had seen were 10 of the 12 calves. I was afraid that if they came across the road again, someone was going to get hurt. I told the sheriff to "shoot to kill." I didn't want any problems.

Well, we moved those gates into the area and tried to round up the herd, but . . . nothing doing. We tried to move them cross-country to the nearest barnyard . . . still, nothing doing. At one point the sickly calf crashed through the ice in a drainage ditch and went down. I figured she was gone.

We stopped for lunch while the sheriff watched and waited for the herd to come across the road again. We spent the rest of the afternoon chasing the calves, with no luck. By the end of the day they were so tired out that they'd run 50 feet to get away from us and then just flop onto the ground. As soon as we got close, they'd just jump up and take off again. Finally, we gave up for the day. We poured a bunch of feed into our makeshift spare-gate pen and went home.

On Thursday morning I got a call from a guy about five miles from me. He had seen my calves trying to get in with his cows. We arrived at his pasture at about the same time. He dropped the wire on the fence, walked in with a bale of hay, and his cows and my calves came running. In about 15 minutes we had them up in the barn. Twenty minutes later they were on my trailer and headed for home.

However, I had only 10 of the 12 calves. The sickly calf that had fallen into the drainage ditch on the second day of the chase was most likely dead. So there was at least one healthy calf still loose.

I got the 10 calves home and secured by noon on Friday. I gave each of them a "kill'em or cure'em" shot of "LA-200."

On Saturday morning I got a call at work from a neighboring farmer who had found one of my calves. He had her in his barn and asked me to come over and get her. I thanked him profusely and ran home to get my trailer.

As I pulled into the drive, I spotted another one of my calves coming through the brush into my neighbor's yard. Unbelievable! I had all 12 of my animals back after a five-day-long chase, and none of them were the worse for the wear! In fact, I swear that sickly calf did better from that day on than any of the others.

This is a true story all the way around. I've got many friends and co-workers to verify it!

When he's not chasing cows, **Dan Rohrer** lives with his wife and daughter, as well as their German Shepherd and tri-colored cat, on a small farm outside of Watertown, Wisconsin. He farms as "a hobby" with his father and his uncle, and raises beef cattle, chickens, cucurbits, corn, soybeans, and alfalfa.

Photo taken in Granite Ledge, Minnesota,
in 1927. The name of the white cow is believed
to have been "Mary." *Photo courtesy of Shirlee Morrison.*

Lulu's Big Day

As told by Lauri D. Goldenhersh

My youngest daughter meekly tapped me on the shoulder, breathing in my face and whispering, "Daddy, Lulu woke me up." Her long brown hair was standing impossibly on end, and she was rubbing her eyes, trying to press the night haze from their lids.

"Go back to bed, sweetheart. I'll get up and feed her when it's light out."

She wasn't convinced. "But Daddy, she's already eating."

Now it was my turn to throw off sleep. "*Wha*...how?" The big red and white Ayrshire certainly couldn't reach the bales from the corral where she slept, and it was still dark out – there was no chance Carlos had come to feed her at 2:00 a.m. "What do you mean, honey?"

"I can hear her munching on the hay by my window."

Oh, boy. The moment I'd feared was upon us - - the cow was loose. I passed Jay to her mother and leapt out from under the covers, landing on both feet.

Living in suburbia with a cow was never the plan. But as it happened, the previous owners of the ranch-style house, both of them contractors, had taken the "ranch" name seriously and had built a one-third of an acre corral in *front* of the hilltop house. We'd assumed they'd kept horses when we first saw it, and kind of shrugged it off. But the view was spectacular, the price was right, and it was only later that we found that the corral had been a strange architectural experiment in mystery kitsch. We had about an acre and a half, and the corral served as a sort of barrier between us and curious joyriders, so we'd left it up.

Now, two years later, my brother Jan was ripping out a corral of his own on a more legitimate 50-acre horse ranch, and had asked us to take care of Lulu for a couple of weeks. Of course we'd agreed. The girls were thrilled, as *none* of their friends had cows in their front yards. Lulu was really kind of cute, kind of like a loud, friendly eating machine. It took me back to my childhood farm, and I was happy to help out, except for one little misgiving.

Jan and I had talked about the fence when he first called, but he was so desperate to place Lulu somewhere, he would probably have agreed to put her in a playpen, had we offered. He had 30 animals to house while he endured major renovation hell, and leaving one with a family member for the price of hay was saving him a bundle. So when I mentioned that the fence had been built inside out, with the rails on the outside of the posts, so they could be pushed out from the inside, he'd pretty much ignored me. He said, "Oh, I'm sure it'll be fine. She's never tried to escape since she's been here, and I don't think she's all that smart."

So much for that. By now I was up, hastily pulling on my jeans, looking for my other shoe. I started to charge through the front door, and caught myself, taking a moment to peer through the curtains on the door's glassed-in upper half. There she was, standing inches from Jay's bedroom window, with hooves on the porch and face buried, searching, in the pile of hay bales dumped there the previous day. Lulu was the image of placid contentment as she munched, and so, when she heard me open the door, I was surprised to see how fast she could suddenly spring into action.

With an eerie bovine squeal, she took off across the yard, crashing through a bougainvillea bush and coming danger-ously close to falling down a steep drop at the edge of the gar-den. As I trotted after her, I could see her round the house and head into the hills behind. They were undeveloped county land - - rolling hills of dry grass that whipped into a frenzied brush fire at the slightest summer spark. About two miles down the dirt road was the riverbed, dry this time of year, and she was headed straight for it. I knew I was going to need backup. She wasn't slowing down, happily trotting through the morning air, and I'd never catch her on foot, even if I could see her through the darkness.

By the time I made my way up the hill and back to the house, it was 3:00 a.m. I grabbed the phone and called my brother. I had to let it ring at least a dozen times before he picked it up, groggy and confused. "Jan," I said. "Get over

here. Your cow has gone AWOL. She's headed for the river."
He mumbled something in horror, but I knew he'd gotten it.
We hung up, and I grabbed my keys, telling my wife where I
thought I was headed.

There was no way to drive directly to the river from our
house. I jumped into my Buick and took the two-mile trek
around the housing development to the reserve area's
entrance, hoping to God that the gate would be open. It was,
and I made my way slowly down the dirt road, trying to avoid
wayward coyotes, which were ubiquitous in this part of town.
Turning left toward the catfish pond, I took the only route I
could imagine Lulu choosing - - it was just easier, and she was
a big girl.

Once I got to the river, I jumped out, flashlight in hand,
looking and listening for everything from snakes to coyotes to
skunks to the vagrants and college students whom we knew
lived and partied here. I'd never been out here in the dark, and
had no idea what to expect. I was really starting to regret not
waiting for Jan. I took a careful look around, and as I heard
nothing and had no idea where to start looking, I got back into
the car and tapped my fingers obsessively on the steering
wheel.

It was only about 25 minutes before he got there, meaning his pickup had practically flown up the interstate. Two of
his ranch hands were with him, and they jumped out quickly
to get the four workhorses out of the trailer. They'd been lucky

that the trailer was still attached to the pickup from last night's show, so loading the sturdy, sometimes truculent beasts had been quick and relatively painless. His guys mounted up, grabbed on, and they were off, ropes in hand. They'd heard Lulu off to our left, and wanted to spot her before the coyotes did. I felt horribly out of place, as I hadn't been on a horse in 10 years, but I climbed on, thinking about bicycles.

By now the morning light was starting to shift, but our flashlights were still a necessity. There was no hope of sneaking up on poor Lulu, surely scared to death, but it was surprising how hard it was to find her at all. She'd somehow worked her way into a thicket of trees, and in the dim light and overlapping branches it was nearly impossible to see where she might be hiding. She was no longer moving around, which was worrisome, but we hadn't heard any big scuffle either.

We searched for more than an hour, in and out of the brush that easily spanned two square miles. The sun was inching its way up the sky in a joyous profusion of glowing color when we heard Rick, Jan's ranch manager, say weakly, "Uh, guys? . . . Gotta surprise for ya." We fought our way into a small, hidden clearing about 10 feet into the trees and discovered that Lulu had safely divided into two unequal portions - - her calf was just starting to wake up, and she was cleaning him gently.

I turned to my older brother, stunned and livid. "Are you *nuts*? You gave us a *pregnant cow*? Were you even going to tell us?"

"What — you didn't know? It's true, we didn't think she'd deliver until after she came home, but I thought you'd figured it out." He tried to look innocent, but knew he'd really screwed up.

"Based on what? Her cravings for pickles? I don't even know what bovine morning sickness looks like. Remember, we may have grown up on a farm, but by the time I came along, we didn't have a lot of livestock. We grew *apples*. Their 'babies' don't require major care."

It was a dumb joke, and we both knew it. But none of us could stop laughing, being so relieved to have found Jan's wayward Ayrshire. Lulu and Lulette, as the calf was immediately dubbed, gazed at us with unflappable disinterest, as they clearly had better things to do. After a reasonable pause as they took care of business, we got both of them up and into the horse trailer. They were going home now, whether mama liked it or not.

When Jan came back for the horses, he brought a box of chocolates for the girls and my wife, who had taken the girls to school while we sorted out the drama. We both knew they'd be heartbroken not to see the baby, and to lose their exotic suburban pet. I was nailing the boards back on the fence when he pulled up, grinning.

"So, how about a horse?"

In my head, my lips were saying, "No, no, and no, thank you." But I said, "Yes," anyway, and made a mental note to go out and buy stronger nails and a new set of boots.

Lauri D. Goldenhersh is a writer of essays and poetry, and is an active web writer and blogger. Her story, a family favorite, is told from the perspective of her father. As the editor of LaurisList.com and Singerpreneur.com, she leads a network of professional classical singers. She also runs and contributes to the blogs "Shoestring Eats: home-based cuisine for the freelancer" and "Bloony," an online diary about her "other" life as a balloon twister.

Columbus Day, 1997

C. R. Lindemer

It was a beautiful autumn day in New England…not a cloud in the sky, with a light breeze blowing. Crisp fall colors were splattered all around, and the bright morning sunshine was streaming down. I spent the morning paying some bills, gathering my husband's shirts from the cleaners, and purchasing a few items from the hardware store. It was a holiday day off from my regular office job. Our babysitter, Celesté, was in charge of the three kids until noon.

We had been at the farm for about two years at that point. We had "fallen in love" with the place from the road on a misty fall day. What we would do with it, other than to plant a small apple orchard was anybody's guess. We'd eventually settled on raising a few beef cattle. And through a casual arrangement, a motley herd of goats and horses were boarded in exchange for some caretaking.

As I was unpacking my duct tape, the phone rang. It was the police. "M'am, your cows are on the golf course." Without revealing my state of alarm, I responded, "Thank you. We'll take care of that."

Celesté was preparing to leave for the rest of the holiday. And my husband, Kevin, was at Boston's Logan Airport. I called him on his mobile phone and exclaimed, "The cows are on the golf course!" Alarmed, he inquired, "Do you want me to come home?" My reply was, "Yes, right NOW!"

Standing next to Kevin at Logan was an astute French business associate named Philippe, who warned Kevin that canceling his flight to Paris in order to chase cows would not be good for his career. Overhearing their conversation, I realized that I was pretty much on my own.

After asking Celesté to "stay put," I jumped into my station wagon and tore down the state highway, careening into the parking lot of a nearby restaurant. Moments later, I found myself sprinting across the two-lane highway and vaulting over the guardrail and into waist-high weeds and poison ivy.

On the golf course, at a glimpse, all appeared eerily calm. Golfers dressed in light-colored clothing were leisurely swinging away with their golf clubs, then strolling onward. The lush green turf was neatly trimmed and tended. It did indeed look like a "holiday."

But standing near the fifth fairway was a Jersey heifer. Thirty feet to the north was an Angus steer, chomping down on the turf. Further over was an all-white cow we had named "Milky Way." These were three of the bovine assortment of "starter cattle" we had purchased from the local livestock auction barn. And mixed in with the cattle was that small herd of mangy goats in the shrubs along the fence. I was thankful not to see the "rescued" Clydesdale.

The golf course manager got off his cart and asked me if I had any ideas on how to evict the animals. I informed him that we needed to look for a break in the fence. And we would then need to coax the "alpha" cow through the break, after which the rest of the animals should theoretically follow.

As the golf course staffers and golfers looked on rather helplessly, I climbed through thorny brambles and shrubs, searching for the ruined portion of the rusty barbed-wire-topped fence. After looking for a few minutes, I located a break in the old fence. I emerged from the center of a large and shaggy 10-foot-tall bush, crushing it from side to side with my hands and feet, and informed the onlookers that I had found "the passage."

Together we chased the "alpha" Angus, and at the critical moment, I yelled, "HEEYAH!" And, as I had predicted, the Angus went galloping through the break in the bushes and fence, followed by all of the cattle and goats.

To the golf course guys, I said, "Thanks for your help" and "Sorry for the trouble," and I disappeared back through the bushes.

As I crossed the boggy pasture toward my house, finally able to "collect myself," I spotted our part-time caretaker, Melvin, walking toward me and carrying a long cattle-chasing stick. He was followed by another guy carrying a similar stick. It was a little late, but it's the thought that counts, right?

Melvin put his arm around me and asked me if I was okay. I told him that I was. But I was standing in a muddy cow pasture, I was hugging "the livestock barn guy," and my "executive" husband was on a plane on his way to France.

Bovine Wistfulness

"Suddenly I became aware that my very best ideas of art had come to me while milking a cow in Iowa."

~ Grant Wood (1891-1942)

American painter, famous for the cultural icon

American Gothic

Milking Cows in Iowa

Arlene Stratman Walker

Brown cows, spotted cows, and dirty-white cows. This assortment made up the motley herd on our family's farm. By watching them I learned that cows could be aggressive, passive, or uncooperative by nature.

Our cows often sensed when it was milking time. They could be seen walking from the grassy pasture up the lane, surrounded on both sides by barbed wire fences.

Typically, barn doors were cut in half horizontally so that the top half could remain open to let fresh air blow through the milking area on mild days. The bottom half remained closed and fastened with a hook, keeping animals from wandering in from the barnyard, except for cats which slept on beds of straw and hung around at milking time for sips of milk.

When Dad opened the bottom half of the barn door at milking time, the cows were supposed to come in. Some cows complied obediently. A few had to be prodded to get moving. Each cow knew her assigned stall and knew enough to put her head through the stanchion, a loose-fitting frame that was closed around the neck to lock it in place and opened again after milking time. The manger along the front of the cows supplied hay for munching during milking. A gutter ran along the back of the cows, where they deposited their body waste at unpredictable times.

After my eleventh birthday, Dad and Mom decided it was time for me to learn how to milk a cow. I already had dreams of going away to college after high school, yet I realized that it was only fair to help with the farm chores, which included milking. My brother, two years younger than I, had already mastered the skill. Refusing to learn how to milk cows would be unthinkable.

I had watched both Dad and Mom milk cows. It looked easy, except at times when a cow made a fuss over one thing or another. Dad assigned one of the more gentle cows as mine to milk. The milking stools in our barn were two scraps of thick wood, one for the single leg and the other for a seat, nailed onto the leg so the stool was a T-shape, hardly designed for comfort. It took some practice to balance one's backside on the seat without falling off. Added to that was learning how to hold a milk bucket between one's knees, all the while trying not to startle the cow during milking.

It took awhile to position myself on the stool with the pail in place, and clean off the cow's udder, before taking hold of two of the cow's four teats. It was not enough just to squeeze the teats in rhythm—squeeze left, squeeze right, squeeze left, squeeze right. The squeeze had to be close to where the teat was connected to the udder in order for the milk to even begin to extract. On my first few tries, the cow turned her head to the right - the side on which we always sat - her big brown eyes expressing a puzzled and nervous look. Then she took steps away from me with her hind legs. I dragged my rustic T-stool in a bit closer, and after awhile she started munching, seeing that I was not giving up on milking her.

Cows have always had ways of pulling stunts. One of them was to give a fast kick with a hind leg when perturbed. If a person was not fast enough in pulling the pail away from a cow's sudden kick, the contents of the milk pail would spill into the gutter.

Another cow trick occurred some Saturday evenings during milking time, just after I had washed my hair and put it up in curlers. The cow I milked had a tail just long enough to hang into the gutter. With her tail wet with urine, she some-times caught me off guard and whipped that stinky wet tail around my head. And that meant washing and curling my hair all over again.

Morning and evening, cold winter days or blistering hot summer days, I took my responsibility in the cow barn. With practice, my milking ability improved, and the warm milk would fill the bucket just a bit higher than before. Milking was complete when no milk remained in the udder of a cow.

Getting up from the wooden milking stool was not as difficult as sitting down, and it was accompanied by the satis-faction of having completed the task. The pail of milk was carried into a small room adjacent to the milking area where there was a cream separator. The milk was poured into a milk can with a strainer on it. The strainer was equipped with a porous pad. Foreign objects that had fallen into the milk bucket during milking were caught on the replaceable pad.

Just before separating, the strained milk was poured into a large steel bowl that fit on top of the separator. A handle on the side of the separator was turned to make a stack of steel disks rotate. The rotating disks, shaped like wide cones, separated the cream from the milk. The fresh cream went through a spout and into a metal can that was stored in the coolest place possible in the days when we had no electricity for refrigeration. Often this place was a tank of cold water. And every few days, a produce truck from town picked up the cream.

Milk separated from the cream emptied out through a spout into pails, to be fed to calves or mixed with feed for the pigs. Our cats, valued for controlling the farm's mouse population, were often treated to a huge pan of skim milk from the separator.

We kept back enough milk for our family's use. And cream. Most of the people who dropped in for coffee or hot tea enjoyed it with our cream. And our freshly whipped cream on homemade desserts was always a treat.

After our farm was wired for electricity, Dad brought in a radio and set it on a shelf he'd made from scrap boards. Laughing, he told us someone told him that music from the radio would make the cows more content during milking. By this time, my younger sister was also helping with the milking. We kids decided that music had more benefits than making contented cows. For us, music made for good entertainment while milking. With Dad and us three kids doing the milking, Mom was able to stay in the house and do her other work.

One afternoon, while listening to a quiz program between songs, we heard Mom's voice on the radio. She gave the correct answer to the trivia question posed by the disc jockey and won two movie tickets. We were so excited to hear our mom talk on the radio, and we were very proud of her.

The work of milking cows was not easy, and I was glad when I could put away my pail and my milking stool for the last time. Now that I think back, I treasure the simple lifestyle that our family had, working and laughing together, and forming a close bond while milking cows.

Arlene Stratman Walker milked cows on her parents' farm in northwest Iowa. She has taught elementary classrooms, English Language Learners, and has been a substitute teacher. Her family includes two grown sons and their wives and four grandchildren. She enjoys traveling, reading, cooking, quilting, and walking.

Warming Your Feet, "Country Style"
Kermit H. Dietrich

In the summers on the farm, during the Depression, we went barefoot. This was partly to save money, but mostly because we preferred the freedom. In September we got our "school shoes," but we often carried them home.

One of our chores in the fall was cow herding. The summer grass pasture had gone dormant, and to conserve the stored forage for the winter months, we herded the cows on grain and stubble fields. The re-growth of grain and native grasses provided forage in September and early October.

When we came home from school, we let the cows out and herded them until suppertime. There wasn't much to do, just keep the cows off the road.

My brother and I amused ourselves by pretending to be Roy Rogers, riding the wildest young cattle, or by playing "mumbly-peg." Mumbly-peg is played by throwing a jack-knife into the ground. It was common then for boys to carry jackknives. They were considered essential tools for carving, cutting strings on corn bundles, and for other farm jobs.

When our feet got cold, there were always warm "cow pies" to stand in. I'm not sure if it was a cure or prevention for Athlete's Foot, but we never had it.

On a recent trip to "Amish Country" in Harmony, Minnesota, we met some barefoot children walking home from school. In the year 2000, they were probably among the fortunate few children who still know how to warm their feet in a cow pasture.

Kermit H. Dietrich is a retired dairy farmer and U.S. Navy submarine veteran living in Waconia, Minnesota. He has taught English as a Second Language and currently volunteers at the Carver County Historical Museum. He is now an artist and enjoys painting.

Hilja and Ed's Place

Robert Darling

My final assignment in the U.S. Air Force was to a base in Wadena, Minnesota, from 1955 to 1957. It was during that time that I was "knocked off my feet" by a one-of-a-kind farmer's daughter named Jane. My "life plan" had not included marrying a country girl, but I just went with my heart. After a brief country courtship, we married the following year, moved back East, and have lived there ever since.

While visiting at the family farm, I observed many things. It was a small dairy farm, with only about 10 cows. None of the work was modernized or mechanized back then. The cows were called into the barn early every morning and again in the evening. "Menne nyt, Menne nyt," Ed would yell, urging them to keep moving forward in his thick Finnish accent. They would all calmly and quietly go to their individual stanchions.

One of the cows was a large, black-and-white spotted Holstein. This cow was always dripping milk as she came into the barn, her udder was so full. Ed would milk her first and usually filled two large pails full of milk. As he milked the cows by hand, the cats would all sit nearby, patiently waiting for him to squirt them some warm milk, which they would lap up with great satisfaction.

Jane's mother, Hilja, was a tiny woman. She would wrap a long strip of white muslin around her head several times to cover her hair when she was in the barn. Ed had a large milking stool and Hilja's was much smaller. Hilja would milk her "share" of the cows. She was tiny, but she could milk just as fast as Ed, and she carried her own heavy buckets when they were full.

Summer milking came with the annoying problem of many large flies buzzing in the barn. So Ed's solution was to tie lengths of baler twine to the ceiling, with loops at the opposite ends, which would then be tied onto the ends of the tails of the cows. This kept them from swishing their dirty tails at Ed and Hilja as they milked the cows. Maybe a lot of dairy farmers do that, but it seemed to be Ed's unique invention.

There was a swamp at the back of the pasture, and the cows liked to stand there in the muck on hot days. Of course that made cleaning off the cows' teats much more difficult, especially if the mud had time to dry before milking.

The cows were about the best "weather forecasters" in the summer. They would sense when rainy weather was coming, and they would run around in the pasture like wild animals. That was when we would go and shut all of the windows in the house and put away any tools left out in the yard.

I often helped out on the family farm, and have worked on farms since then, but from those early observations of the labors of my in-laws, I gained an awesome respect for our hard-working dairy farmers.

Robert Darling worked at his family-owned service station and garage for many years and is now the custodian at Mt. Calvary Lutheran Church in Acton, Massachusetts. He enjoys sailing, fishing on the ocean, golfing, bowling, and camping. Bob and Jane have been blessed with five sons, one daughter, and many grandchildren.

Learning to Walk

Allen Doyle

What is special to me is to see a newborn calf stand up for the first time on all four feet.

A calf will try to stand right from the start, but they always slide around and don't get very far. The slippery calf just flounders, first its front feet are up and ready, but its back legs aren't too steady. Down it goes!

Over she goes, time and again, and then she just lies there with a puzzled and tired look. But with a sparkle in her eyes and a look of determination, she springs up on all fours and does it just right! She may wobble and weave back and forth, but then she's up, resting on the ground no longer.

Slowly, the calf walks toward her mother, but the cow walks past the calf for now. When that calf is hungry for a drink, she'll drink her fill of warm milk, and then run all around showing off her new skill.

Allen Doyle enjoys writing, including poetry, and restoring old cars. He has restored three Model A Fords: 1928, 1930, and 1931. A difficult turn of events resulted in the sale of his entire herd of cattle. He prays for better days in the state of New York.

Curious Calf © Patti Blair www.OneHeartArtworks.com

Always a Cowgirl

Verda Vanecek Doop

I met Johnny, the love of my life, when I was 19 and he was 21. After a six-week courtship we married, on July 5, 1927. We started our married life with so little – only healthy bodies, a few head of cattle, and a willingness to work.

We worked at any odd jobs we could find to make ends meet. And after living with Johnny's parents for two and a half years, we bought our first ranch in Trinity, Texas. We began buying more cows from local farmers and ranchers. Some we eventually sold at the Fort Worth stockyards, others we kept, and our small herd of cattle increased right along. It didn't set well with me when Johnny traded something one time for a yoke of oxen. But he sold the oxen (without the yoke) a few days later for a profit. I still have that yoke!

Eventually we bought more land from a couple who moved to Kansas. Then a big lumber company in our town began selling off their assets and closed down their operations. We leased 8,000 acres of pastureland from the lumber company when it shut down and bought an entire herd of cattle to run on that land. Our ranch was steadily growing.

That vast pastureland had two creeks running through it, and when we had heavy rains, the creeks would overflow and cover the countryside. The first time that happened we went to check on our cattle to see if any were stranded by the rising water. I was riding our big black horse, Beauty, and Johnny was riding Tony. We rode up to that flooded creek and, to me, it looked like the Pacific Ocean! I was frantic, and said "You don't think I'm going to ride into that, do you?" Johnny just rode into the water and said, "Give your horse the loose reins and come on." I did what he said, and when Beauty went to swimming, my heart was in my mouth, and I just held on.

Another time one of our bulls – a very mean one! – escaped our pasture and was found quite a distance from our ranch. We took the truck, and Johnny told me how to position it in order for him and a helper to load the bull. They got ropes on the bull, but he braced for an attack when he saw the truck. He rammed the side of the truck very hard about three or four times, and I was sure he was going to get to me. Even after the men were able to get the bull into the truck, he was still lurching and trying to ram the cab of the truck. Johnny kept shouting, "Don't move!" He later praised me for managing to remain so calm in that uncertain situation.

Some of my fondest memories of my ranching days are from those times when friends and neighbors came for roundups when we branded our cattle. Time has changed the ways in which this was done. In those days we had an "army" of riders and stock dogs to round up and herd the cattle into the corral. There was no such thing as a calf table for branding at that time. Calves were roped in the pens and tied down.

Sometimes it took several men to handle a calf – and then some got their britches kicked off! The cattle were very wild in those days, as they ranged in the river bottoms and heavily wooded areas and seldom saw anyone until roundup time.

The branding irons were heated by a pine knot fire, as there were no propane tanks like we have today. During my "cowboy days" I handed many hot branding irons through the fence. It was hard work, and at noon the crew didn't go to Dairy Queen for hamburgers. We wives would cook and pack up the food and take it to them. It was hard work, but we all enjoyed it, for every roundup was like a "Wild West Rodeo."

We eventually downsized our operation, and Johnny died when he was only 64.

I still have my own herd of cattle, and even into my 90s, I insisted on going along to watch my son work "my cattle." My daughter-in-law still drives me out on late afternoons so I can sit and watch my cattle graze in the pasture. I will always love to reminisce about my life as a rancher's wife in the Lone Star State.

Verda Vanecek Doop is 101 years old and lives with her son and her daughter-in-law in Trinity, Texas, on the same ranch where these events took place.

Sources

http://www.midwestdairy.com
http://www.padairy.org/
http://www.vadairyprincess.org/
http://www.national4-hheadquarters.gov/
http://upload.wikimedia.org/wikipedia/commons/f/f7/
    Burgess-cow.jpg
Josh Billings' Old Farmer's Allminax 1870-1879 with
    Comic Illustrations. G.W. Dillingham Co., 1902.

Do you have a **True Cow Tale**?

Submit your story (approximately 500-1500 words long), for the possibility of publication in a future edition to:

True Cow Tales
P.O. Box 961
Groton, MA 01450
U.S.A.

Please make sure to enclose your contact information. You will be contacted if your story is selected for publication.

or send via e-mail to: crlindemer@gmail.com
(*Note:* Please submit stories in the body of the e-mail - not as an attachment. *Thank you!*)

Breinigsville, PA USA
16 September 2009
224225BV00001B/1/P